AMERICAN NATURE GUIDES
HERBS

AMERICAN NATURE GUIDES
HERBS

ANNA KRUGER

SMITHMARK

This edition first published by
SMITHMARK Publishers Inc.,
112 Madison Avenue, New York 10016

Published in England by Dragon's World Ltd,
Limpsfield and London

Editor: Diana Steedman
Designer: Ann Doolan
Art Director: Dave Allen
Editorial Director: Pippa Rubinstein

SMITHMARK Books are available for bulk purchase for
sales promotions and premium use. For details write or
telephone the Manager of Special Sales, SMITHMARK
Publishers Inc., 112 Madison Avenue, New York,
New York 10016.
(212) 532-6600

ISBN 0 8317 6952 1

Printed in Singapore

CONTENTS

Introduction   6

Glossary   7

A–Z HERBAL   10

Index   191

Introduction

What is a herb?

The term herb can describe any plant, or part of a plant, that is used for its medicinal, culinary or aromatic qualities. The range of plants that this definition encompasses changes according to your perspective. In urban areas, experience of herbs may be limited to the purely culinary, whereas to indigenous peoples, who have always lived close to nature, virtually any plant could be classified as a herb.

Throughout the history of our civilization, plants have provided us with food and medicine. Fossilized mustard, wild rose hips, and yarrow pollen – all of them herbs in current medicinal usage – have been found in neolithic excavations, which suggest that herbal knowledge is thousands of years old. Today, our connection with the natural world may be limited to brief trips to the country and holidays by the sea, but we still retain something of our ancestors' herbal lore. Most people are aware that dock leaves soothe the sting of nettles and many of us still participate in the old-established ritual of gathering blackberries from the wild in early autumn. Like us, our rural forebears made the berries into jellies, pies and wine, but, unlike us, they probably had neither the means, nor the access, to medical help. For them, blackberry syrup was a home remedy for sore throats; they applied the fresh leaves to burns and scalds, and drank a tea of the leaves and root bark for diarrhoea and dysentery. Herbal history is also steeped in superstition, magic and mysticism, and although we now live in an age of technological wizardry, we continue, nevertheless, to honour some ancient, pagan rituals. Our Christmas tradition of kissing under the mistletoe, for example, has its origins in ancient Druidic fertility rites.

Herbs in the wild

Many herbs are now fast disappearing from the wild, principally on account of the destruction of the plants' natural habitats and the introduction of modern farming methods which rely on chemical fertilizers. To safeguard vulnerable wild herbs from further damage, never uproot a whole wild plant and take as few leaves, flowers, and especially seeds, as possible. Also, make sure that you have clearly identified any wild herb that you may wish to eat or use medicinally. Plants are potent medicines and some are poisonous: the consequences of mistaking foxglove leaves for comfrey, for example, can be serious. If you are unfamiliar with wild herbs, you should first consult a reliable, comprehensive guide, preferably with photographs.

Glossary

Aerial part Any part of a plant that grows above ground.

Annual A plant that completes its life cycle from seed to maturity and death in one growing season.

Axil The angle formed between the main stem and a branch, leaf stalk or flowering stem.

Biennial A plant that completes its life cycle from seed to maturity and death over two growing seasons. Flowering and fruiting often occur in the second year.

Deciduous A plant or tree that loses its leaves in autumn.

Floret A small flower, part of a head or cluster.

Herb A plant or part of a plant that is valued for its medicinal, culinary or aromatic properties.

Herbaceous A plant that is not woody and has leafy growth which dies down in winter.

Leaflet A segment of a compound leaf.

Lobe A rounded segment of a leaf.

Perennial A plant that lives for three or more growing seasons.

Rhizome An underground stem, usually growing horizontally, that bears shoots above and roots beneath.

Root A plant's main underground storage organ that anchors it in the ground.

Rootstock A short, thick rhizome, especially one that is not horizontal but more or less erect.

Runner A trailing stem that grows along the ground and produces roots.

Sepal A leaf-like part, usually green, that sheaths a flower before it opens.

Stamen The male, pollen-bearing part of a flower.

Taproot A long, fleshy storage root that grows vertically.

Tuber A swollen underground storage organ, growing from a stem or root.

Terminal Growing at the top.

Umbel A flat-topped or umbrella-shaped flower cluster with all the flower stalks radiating from a common point.

Whorl A circular arrangement, at the same level on a stem, of three or more leaves or flowers.

Elliptic

Linear

Lanceolate

Oblong

Obovate

Ovate

Palmate

Pinnate

Dentate

Entire

Incised

Lobed

Serrate

Aconite

Aconitum napellus

Monkshood, wolf's bane, helmet flower

Habitat Native to mountainous regions of Europe, particularly the Swiss Alps and the Pyrenees. Grows wild in open woods and on wooded mountain slopes, preferring moist soils and shade. Cultivated in Europe and North America.

Description Herbaceous perennial but roots produce flowers in alternate years. Erect stem to 90cm (3ft) with dark green, glossy, palmate leaves that have jagged teeth. Distinctive purple, violet or blue flowers appear in terminal spikes during summer and autumn. The upper petal (actually a sepal) takes the form of a hood or helmet that fits closely over the rest of the flower. The root is fleshy and turnip-shaped. **Parts used**: whole plant, root.

History Aconite, especially the root, contains a group of deadly poisonous alkaloids. According to Greek myth, the plant acquired its venom from the foaming mouth of the three-headed dog Cerberus, who guarded the entrance to Hades. The herb's common name, wolf's bane, is thought to refer to an old method of killing wolves – either with arrows dipped in poisonous aconite juice, or in traps smeared with it.

Aconite is a hallucinogen that produces tingling sensations in the limbs. On account of these powerful effects, it was reputedly a favourite witches' herb and was, along with belladonna, the principal ingredient of their celebrated 'flying ointment'. A drug prepared from aconite was once used to relieve the pain of neuralgia and sciatica, but imprecise dosages led to fatalities and the drug was withdrawn.

CAUTION All parts of the plant are poisonous.

Agrimony

Agrimonia eupatoria

Church steeples, cocklebur

Habitat Widespread throughout Europe, in parts of Asia, and in North America, especially the mountain slopes of southern California and in Arizona. Grows on waste ground, roadsides, along field edges and in hedgerows.

Description Graceful perennial with downy to rough, reddish stems from 30–60cm (1–2ft). Its numerous leaves divide into oblong, toothed, deep green and downy pairs with a slight apple scent. Yellow, aromatic five-petalled flowers appear from June to August, packed closely together in elongated spikes. They are followed by bristly, hooked seeds.

Parts used: aerial parts, dried root.

History The Anglo-Saxons considered agrimony an excellent wound-healing herb and employed it for snake bites. For internal bleeding, a powerful concoction of the pounded fresh leaves, human blood, and the flesh of frogs was recommended. Agrimony's long association with magic is also clearly reflected in the Medieval belief that a person who slept with agrimony under the pillow would not wake up until the herb was removed. In 15th-century France, agrimony was an important ingredient of a healing water known as *arquebusade* that was used to treat arquebus wounds. In 16th-century England, wounds were commonly treated with a mixture of agrimony, mugwort and vinegar.

Sixteenth-century herbalists recommended agrimony for liver problems and modern herbalists still consider the herb useful for gallstones. Agrimony has astringent properties and is employed in folk medicine to speed up the healing of wounds. Agrimony water was once taken as a soothing gargle by singers and public speakers.

Alfalfa

Medicago sativa

Lucerne, buffalo herb

Habitat Native to the Mediterranean and western Asia, naturalized in North America. Found wild on the edges of fields and in low-lying valleys as an escape from cultivation. This plant is widely cultivated as far afield as Iran and Peru as a fodder crop.

Description Perennial with a deep taproot penetrating to a depth of 9–30m (30–100ft) and an upright, extensively branched stem from 30cm–1m (1–3ft) in height. Leaves are oval, grouped in threes, and growth is abundant. Numerous erect spikes of blue or violet flowers that resemble clover appear from June to August followed by hairy seed pods in coiled spirals. **Parts used**: leaf, sprouted seed.

History Alfalfa has been grown in the Middle East since ancient times as a fodder crop for Arab horses. During the 17th century the plant acquired its common name, lucerne, from the Latin for lamp – a reference to its luminous seeds. Medicinally, alfalfa tea was drunk to improve the appetite, while its diuretic action is helpful for urinary problems and water retention. Native Americans reputedly took alfalfa seed to procure abortions.

Alfalfa seeds are highly nutritious and contain vitamins C, B_1, B_2, K, chlorophyll, and amino acids. When the seeds are sprouted the vitamin concentration increases, making alfalfa an excellent source of nutrients. Alfalfa can be sprouted easily at home, or bought ready sprouted from greengrocers and health food stores. Use the sprouts in salads or sandwiches.

Allspice

Pimenta dioica, Pimenta officinalis

Jamaica pepper, myrtle pepper

Habitat Native to the West Indies, especially Jamaica, Central America and Mexico. Now grown commercially in many tropical countries including Indonesia. Prefers hilly areas on limestone soils. In temperate northern zones the tree can be grown under glass but will not flower.

Description Evergreen tree resembling the myrtle at 12m (40ft) with large, leathery, glossy green leaves 12.5cm (5in) long and prominently veined on the underside. Tree bears fruit after three years and small white flowers appear from June to August. These are followed by bunches of green berries that ripen to dark brown and look like large peppercorns. **Parts used**: berries.

History Allspice is not a mixture of several different spices but the fruit of a tropical Caribbean tree. The name allspice was coined in the late 17th century to describe its taste – a combination of cinnamon, cloves, nutmeg and pepper. Jamaica supplies most of the world demand, hence the common name Jamaica pepper, and the island's allspice woods are known as Pimento walks.

Allspice contains a pungent volatile oil, formerly known as oil of Pimento and once employed medicinally for indigestion and flatulence. Today, the principal use of allspice is culinary although, like other common kitchen spices, allspice does alleviate wind and colic. Whole allspice is commonly employed in pickling, while the ground spice is usually added to a wide variety of sweet dishes.

Almond

Prunus dulcis, Prunus amygdalus

Sweet almond

Habitat Native to the eastern Mediterranean, especially
Jordan, Iran and the Middle East. Introduced to southern
Europe and widely cultivated in all countries bordering on the
Mediterranean, particularly Spain and Italy. Also cultivated in
California. Prefers sun and well-drained soil.

Description Spreading tree to 7m (20ft) with smooth, pale–
coloured branches. In common with other trees in this family
(cherry, peach and plum), pink or white blossom appears
before the first leaves from mid to late spring. The flowers are
solitary and stalkless; the leaves oval, pointed at the end and
finely toothed. Fruit is dull green with an outer covering that
toughens when ripe then splits to reveal the familiar nuts in
their yellowish, pitted shells. **Parts used**: nuts, oil.

History The almond has been cultivated in the Middle East
for centuries and is mentioned in the Bible. According to
Greek mythology, the gods took pity on Phyllis, a beautiful
nymph deserted by her lover Demophoon, and transformed
her into a flowering almond. The Greeks introduced
the tree to Europe and in Elizabethan times ground
almonds were widely used in cooking. In
European cuisine almonds may be
served with fish, but they are
more extensively used in Near
and Middle Eastern
cookery.

Almonds yield a
soothing and softening
oil that is said to be
helpful for alleviating
itchy skin conditions,
such as eczema.
The oil is popular
with masseuses
and aromatherapists
as it is light, easily
absorbed, and makes
an excellent carrier oil
for essential oils.
Ground almonds are also beneficial
to the skin and make a cleansing
and softening facial scrub.

Aloe

Aloe vera

Barbados aloes, Curaçao aloes

Habitat Found wild in East and South Africa. Naturalized in North Africa, the Caribbean, and parts of the Mediterranean. Widely cultivated in the West Indies, Africa, Texas and Florida. Prefers stony, well-drained soil and a dry, sunny climate. Commonly grown as a houseplant.

Description Succulent perennial plant belonging to the lily family, from 30–150cm (1–5ft). The base of the plant is a rosette of fleshy, narrow, lance-shaped leaves, 30–60cm (1–2ft) in length with prickly edges and whitish green on both sides. Clusters of yellow or orange-red flowers grow at the end of long stalks rising from the rosette and appear throughout most of the year. The stems may be woody. **Parts used**: fresh or dried juice from the cut leaves.

History *Aloe vera* has been used medicinally since 400 BC. The ancient Greeks considered it a valuable purgative and the gel was applied to wounds to speed up the healing process. Today the gelatinous juice of the aloe is rarely used internally and is most commonly employed externally for its remarkable ability to heal burns, sunburn, dermatitis, eczema, and poison-ivy rash. In the USA, aloe has become an essential first-aid remedy and many households keep an aloe plant on the windowsill. For minor burns or skin rashes, break off a leaf and apply the gel.

Growing tips Aloe needs a minimum temperature of 5°C (41°F) and a sunny position. It grows well indoors in warm, dry rooms and requires little water. Propagate from off-shoots planted in gritty or sandy soil.

Amaranth

Amaranthus hypochondriacus

Love-lies-bleeding, lady bleeding, prince's feather

Habitat Native to the tropics and Central American states. Found wild on both waste ground and cultivated land. One of a number of species grown horticulturally.

Description Tall annual herb with a stout, erect, branched stem from 1–1.5m (3–5ft). The leaves are dull green with purple-red spots. Deeply veined on the underside, they are oval and taper to a point. Dense clusters of small crimson to blood-red flowers appear in a long, upright spikes in late summer. **Part used**: leaves.

History Amaranth takes its name from the Greek *amaranton*, meaning unwithering, because the flowers retain their shape and colour when dried. In ancient Greece the flower was sacred to Ephesian Artemis and regarded as a symbol of constancy and fidelity.

Medicinally, amaranth gained favour in the 17th century when the Doctrine of Signature prevailed. To adherents of this doctrine, the bright crimson of the flowers signified blood – a clear indication that the plant would stop any kind of bleeding. The herb does in fact possess astringent properties and herbalists have recommended an amaranth infusion for diarrhoea and as a mouthwash for ulcers. Amaranth has also been employed to check excessive menstrual flow. The young leaves were once eaten as a vegetable.

American Cranesbill

GERANIACEAE

Geranium maculatum

Wild geranium, spotted cranesbill

Habitat Native to North America, especially the eastern USA. Found wild in woodlands and on low ground as far north as Newfoundland.

Description Erect hairy plant to 60cm (2ft) with long-stalked leaves divided into five lobes and deeply incised. The leaves are coarsely toothed and become spotted with age. Large flowers with pale to rose-purple petals, veined at the base, grow in pairs from late spring to late summer followed by beaked seed capsules. The root is stout, brown externally and white inside. **Part used**: rootstock.

History The botanical name *Geranium* refers to the beaked seeds of the plant that were likened to the bill of the crane. *Maculata* means spotted and refers to the white blotches that appear on the leaves as they age. American cranesbill is a traditional Native American herb that was once listed in the US Pharmacopeia. The tannins in the root are responsible for its diuretic action and herbalists recommend the plant for diarrhoea and haemorrhoids. A mouthwash of the herb is also helpful for sore throats, mouth ulcers, and gum infections, while the dried and powdered root has been applied to wounds to stop bleeding.

Angelica

Angelica archangelica

Garden angelica, European angelica

Habitat Originated in Asia or northern Europe. Grows wild in cooler northern European countries as an escape and quickly establishes itself in damp meadows, and on riverbanks. Widely cultivated.

Description Tall, celery-like biennial or perennial herb to 2m (6ft). The stem is stout, hollow, and fluted, purplish at the base and branching near the top. The broad, bright green leaves are sheathed at the base, pinnate in form, deeply indented and subdivided. Small flowers, greenish white and sweet smelling, grow in large round umbels from mid-summer to early autumn. They are succeeded by aromatic, pale yellow seeds. **Parts used**: stems, leaves, root, seeds.

History In Medieval times, angelica was credited with the power to ward off evil spirits and witches. People wore necklaces of angelica leaves and steeped the roots to make holy water. During the Great Plague of the 17th century it was used as a protection against infection. According to Christian legend, an angel revealed angelica's protective powers, and the plant reputedly blooms on the feast day of Michael the Archangel.

Angelica's green stems have long been candied and used to decorate cakes, while the aromatic seeds have flavoured liqueurs and cordials since the Middle Ages. Medicinally, angelica root and leaves have digestive and expectorant properties.

Growing tips Use fresh seed and sow in rich soil in a damp spot. Thin to 1m (3ft).

Aniseed

Pimpinella anisum

Anise

Habitat Native of Egypt, Greece and the eastern
Mediterranean. Grows on dry, poor soils in sunny situations.
Widely cultivated in many warm climates, particularly the
southern Mediterranean, North Africa, India, Turkey, and
parts of South America.

Description Aromatic annual with erect stems to 60cm (2ft).
The long-stalked, bright-green leaves, like coriander, are lobed
and kidney-shaped at the base of the plant, becoming feathery
and finely incised further up the stem. Numerous dainty white
to yellowish-white flowers grow in sparse umbels during July
and August followed by oval, hairy, brown, ribbed seeds. The
seeds have a sweet taste. **Part used**: seed.

History Aniseed was cultivated by the ancient Egyptians,
Greeks, and Romans, and introduced into Central Europe
during the Middle Ages. In Roman times anise was grown for
its digestive properties and the seed was made into a spiced
cake, possibly the precursor
of the traditional wedding
cake, that the Romans ate
to help with digestion
after a rich feast. In many
regional Indian cuisines, too,
aniseed forms part of *paan*, a
seed mixture chewed after a spicy
meal to prevent flatulence and
sweeten the breath.

Aniseed has long been used
to flavour cakes and bread in
Eastern Europe, but its principal
use is in
aniseed-
based liqueurs
such as *Anisette*,
Pernod and *Ouzo*.

Medicinally, aniseed
has a mild expectorant
and antibiotic action. The seeds
were once an ingredient of asthma
powders and herbalists may still
recommend them for bronchitis and
tight, dry coughs.

Arnica

Arnica montana

Leopard's bane, mountain tobacco, mountain daisy

Habitat Grows wild in the mountain pastures and woodlands of Central Europe and Siberia at altitudes of 1200–2800m (4000–9000ft). Naturalized in North America and related species are also found in Canada and western USA. Prefers sandy or loamy soils in sunny situations. This plant is protected and cultivated in parts of Central Europe for use in homeopathic preparations.

Description Aromatic perennial with a flat rosette of oval, downy, toothed, bright green leaves that rests on the ground. The stem is 30–60cm (1–2ft), hairy, with one to two pairs of smaller, opposite, leaves without stalks. Daisy-like yellow-orange flowers that are pleasantly scented appear from mid- to late summer. The petals are covered with fine, silky hairs and are notched at the tip. **Part used**: flower heads.

History In mountainous areas of Europe, arnica is a folk remedy for bruises and sprains. It allegedly grows on lower mountain slopes, within easy reach of those who have fallen from the peaks. Applied externally, arnica ointment reduces inflammation, but internally, the herb can irritate the digestive system, unless it is used in homeopathic dosage. This plant is perhaps the best-known of all the homeopathic remedies and is also considered an excellent first-aid remedy for shock. Arnica must not be used where the skin is broken. Dried arnica leaves were once smoked as a tobacco substitute.

Growing tips Sow indoors or in a cold frame in a peaty or loamy soil mixed with sand in early spring. Plant out in a sunny, sheltered position.

Arrowroot

Maranta arundinaceae

Maranta starch, Indian arrowroot

Habitat Native to the West Indies and tropical America from Mexico south to Brazil. Introduced to Southeast Asia, India, and Africa and cultivated commercially on a small scale.

Description Perennial on a creeping rhizome with scaly, fleshy tubers. The stems are reed-like and grow to 2m (6ft) with oval leaves that are sheathed at the base and smooth. Pairs of cream-coloured flowers appear at the ends of the long stems. **Part used:** rhizome.

History The mashed rhizome was applied to speed up the healing of arrow wounds and bites, hence the plant's common name.

Asparagus

Asparagus officinalis

Garden asparagus, sparrow grass

Habitat Found wild from Britain to Central Asia on coasts and sandy ground, in woods and hedgerows.

Description Perennial on short rootstock with edible greenish-pink fleshy shoots that reach 1–3m (3–9ft) on maturing. They bear needle-like leaves that are really branches: the leaves are scaly and inconspicuous. Small, greenish-white, bell-shaped flowers appear in late spring to early summer, followed by a small, red berry. **Parts used**: root and young stems.

History Asparagus, which has been cultivated for over 2000 years, acts on the kidneys and is a very effective natural diuretic.

Avens

Geum urbanum

Herb Bennet, wood avens

Habitat Native to Europe and common also in Russia and Central Asia. Widespread in hedgerows, mixed woodland, and wood edges on moist soil.

Description Perennial with branched, slender, downy stems, to 30cm (12in). The larger, stalked, deep green basal leaves are three-lobed with toothed edges, and the smaller, upper leaves are stalkless. Solitary yellow flowers with five petals appear from late spring to early autumn followed by distinctive fruiting heads that terminate in a hook. The tough, fibrous root is 3–7cm (1–3in) long and smells of cloves. **Parts used**: root, leaves.

History In Medieval times avens was known as *Herba benedicta* and considered a blessed herb. Its three-lobed leaves were held to signify the Holy Trinity, while the five petals of the flowers symbolized the wounds of Christ. Later the Latin name was changed to St Benedict's herb, and Herb Bennet is a further corruption. Avens' root is aromatic and gives off a clove-like smell that, according to Medieval folklore, would drive away evil spirits. The roots became indispensable in the home, not only for their powers of exorcism, but also because the strong scent repelled moths, and it was customary to lay the roots amongst bed linen and hang them in cupboards. Avens' root was an inexpensive substitute for cloves and a popular flavouring for home-brewed ale.

Herbalists since Paracelsus have valued the bitter, tonic properties of avens for treating digestive problems and to promote appetite. Its astringent and antiseptic action is considered helpful for diarrhoea, haemorrhoids, and to check bleeding.

Balm

Melissa officinalis

Lemon balm, common balm

Habitat Native to South and Central Europe, North Africa and western Asia. Introduced and widespread in northern temperate zones, and often found wild as an escape. Naturalized in the south of England. Cultivated commercially and as a garden plant. Prefers rich, moist soil and sun.
Description Perennial similar to a bushy mint and very sweet smelling. Stems square and slightly hairy from 30–80cm (12–32in), branched at the top and sometimes straggly. The greenish-yellow leaves are oval to heart-shaped at the base, coarsely serrate, and give off a sweet lemon scent when bruised. Small clusters of flowers appear in the axils from late summer to mid autumn, yellowish at first but often changing to pale pink or white. **Part used**: leaves.
History Balm, which takes its botanical name from the Greek for bee, has been a popular Mediterranean bee plant for over 2000 years. According to folk-lore, bees would never leave a garden where balm grew.

Balm was a favourite remedy of the old Arabic physicians who considered it a tonic for the heart, and uplifting to the spirits. Some six centuries later, Culpeper continued to recommend balm for its anti-depressant effect. Today, tests have confirmed that balm has a soothing and sedative action, and the essential oil is said to relieve anxiety and nervous headaches. Balm tea promotes sweating and is a traditional remedy for feverish colds.

Add the fresh leaves to summer wine cups and jellies.

Balmony

Chelone glabra

Turtlebloom, turtlehead

Habitat Native to North America from Newfoundland south
to Florida and west to Texas. Found on low-lying marshy
ground, in damp thickets, and on stream and river banks.
Description Beautiful perennial with an erect, square stem
to 120cm (2–4ft). The opposite, shiny leaves are narrow with
serrated edges and taper to a point. They have a tea-like smell.
Short dense spikes of two-lipped, scentless, white flowers
tinged with pink appear in late summer, from July to
September. **Part used**: leaves.
History Balmony takes its botanical name, *chelone*, from the
Greek for tortoise, on account of the flowers resembling a
turtle's head. Balmony is a traditional Native American herb,
and the bitter-tasting leaves were taken for their tonic effect on
the digestion as well as their laxative properties.

Today herbalists consider balmony a valuable bitter tonic
that has a beneficial action on the liver and gall bladder,
and may recommend it for gallstones. The herb may also be
prescribed for general intestinal problems, and it is
particularly appropriate for
treating children with
roundworms and
threadworms.
Internally, balmony has
a gentle laxative action.
Externally, an
ointment of
the fresh
leaves has
been used
to treat
haemorrhoids
and ulcers.

Barberry

BERBERIDACEAE

Berberis vulgaris

European barberry, pepperidge bush

Habitat Native to Europe and eastward to East Asia.
Naturalized in the north-eastern USA from Nova Scotia south
to Pennsylvania and westward to Iowa in light woodland and
hedgerows. Now scarce in the wild.

Description Deciduous, branched shrub to 2m (7ft) with
greyish woody stems and three sharp spines at the branch
nodes. The pale green, glossy leaves are spoon-shaped with
fine, sharp teeth. Small bright yellow flowers hang from the
branches in clusters from mid-spring, followed by orange-red,
oblong berries. **Parts used**: root bark, ripe fruit.

History Barberry's medicinal properties were known to the
ancient Egyptians who employed the plant to protect them
from infectious diseases. During the Middle Ages, barberry
was regarded as a tonic, an antiseptic, and also taken as a
laxative. Native Americans valued the root bark and drank a
tea for its restorative effect following illness.

The active ingredients of the bark, particularly berberine,
possess antibacterial properties that are
helpful for treating infection, and the
root has a beneficial
action on the
intestines. The
ripe berries, which
are astringent
and mildly
anaesthetic, may
be crushed and
strained to
making a soothing
gargle for sore throats.
Berberine, however, can
stimulate the uterus so
the herb must be avoided
during pregnancy.

Barberry's sharp-tasting
fruits resemble cranberries and are
traditionally made into jams, jellies
and preserves.

Basil

Ocimum basilicum

Sweet basil, garden basil

Habitat Native to India, southern Asia and Middle East. Cultivated extensively in southern, central and eastern Europe, North Africa, and in the USA, particularly California.

Description Very aromatic, bushy annual from 30–60cm (1–2ft) with branching stems that bear tender, light green, oval leaves with slightly toothed margins. Clusters of small, white, two-lipped flowers appear towards the tops of the stems from mid- to late summer. One hybrid has purple-tinged leaves and pink flowers. **Part used**: leaves.

History Basil was introduced to Europe from India where it was once customary in Hindu homes to place a sprig of basil on the dead before burial to ensure their safe passage to the next world. According to Medieval superstition, scorpions liked to hide beneath pots of basil, and if a sprig was left under the pot it would hatch into a scorpion. Basil continued to inspire fear well into the 17th century when it was believed that taking snuff made from the powdered leaves would allow scorpions to nest in your brain.

Basil's principal use is culinary. The pungent fresh leaves are the principal ingredient of the classic Italian pasta sauce, *pesto Genovese*, and basil's flavour is particularly compatible with tomatoes. Hot basil tea is said to alleviate indigestion and stomach cramps. The dried, powdered herb was once taken as snuff to clear the head in cases of headache or colds.

Growing tips Sow seed indoors in late spring and plant outside in early summer in rich, well-drained soil in a sunny, sheltered position. Mist the leaves and water frequently in hot weather.

Bay

Laurus nobilis

Sweet bay, sweet laurel

Habitat Originated in Asia Minor and well-established in the Mediterranean. Grows wild in high, sheltered, sunny valleys with rich soil. European variety usually grown as a bush. Widely cultivated commercially in the Mediterranean, North Africa, North and Central America.

Description Evergreen tree with shiny, grey bark that may grow to over 30m (45ft) in ideal conditions but is usually restricted to 2m (6ft). The glossy, dark green, leathery leaves are aromatic when crushed, oval in shape and pointed at both ends. From late spring to early autumn clusters of small yellow-white flowers appear in the leaf axils, followed by dark purple berries resembling small olives. **Part used**: leaves.

History In classical times Bay was sacred to the sun-god Apollo who wore a crown of its leaves, a practice later adopted to glorify emperors, athletes, victors, and scholars. The custom persists today in the British tradition of appointing a Poet Laureate – a poet crowned with laurel.

Bay is virtually indispensable in French and Mediterranean cooking, and is one of the ingredients of *bouquet garni*. Bay's medicinal applications included inducing abortions, and curing snakebites, urinary problems, and rheumatism. Today, herbalists still consider bay-leaf oil an effective rub for stiff or rheumatic joints.

Growing tips Propagation from cuttings is difficult and rooting may take up to nine months. Young nursery trees can be planted directly in the garden, or in tubs with rich soil, plus sand. Choose a sunny, sheltered position.

Bayberry

Myrica cerifera

Wax myrtle, candleberry

Habitat Native to eastern USA, from New Jersey south to Florida and Texas. Found on sandy soils around coastal marshes, on stream banks, and in meadows.

Description An evergreen shrub or a small tree which grows up to 11m (35ft) tall, much branched and covered with smooth, greyish bark. The leaves are lance-shaped and are dotted with resinous glands. They are fragrant when bruised. In spring yellowish, catkin-like flowers appear, with the male and female flowers on separate plants. These are followed by groups of greyish or greenish-white crusty, waxen berries.

Parts used: wax, root bark.

History Bayberry tea, made from the root bark, is a traditional remedy for sore throats and diarrhoea on account of its astringency. Chewing the bark was also said to relieve toothache. A snuff made from the powdered bark was taken as a decongestant, while poultices of the fresh bark were applied to ulcers and sores. Today, bayberry bark is seldom employed medicinally. In cosmetic terms, a decoction of the root bark was made into an astringent skin lotion.

The berries furnish a fine, light-greenish, scented wax which is extracted by boiling the berries in water and skimming the solidified wax from the surface. Early American settlers collected large quantities of the berries and made the wax into candles and soap, hence the herb's common name candleberry.

Bearberry

Arctostaphylos uva-ursi

Bears' grape, mountain box

Habitat Found in areas with cooler climates, including Scotland, northern Europe and the northern USA as far south as northern California. Prefers moors and coniferous woodland with rocky or sandy soils. Related species are cultivated as garden ornamentals.

Description Low, trailing evergreen shrub to 15cm (6in) that has many branches covered with dark flakey bark. The leathery, dark green leaves form thick mats and are rounded at the apex. Drooping stems of bell-shaped white, pink or reddish-tinged flowers appear in spring that resemble those of heather. They are followed in autumn by bright red currant-sized, shining berries. **Part used**: leaves.

History Bearberry has been important medicinally since the 13th century. In European and Native American herbal medicine, the leaves, which are powerfully astringent and antiseptic, have long been valued for their tonic action on the kidneys, and are traditionally recommended for kidney stones, and urinary infections such as cystitis. Native Americans applied the fresh leaves to strained muscles, while a wash of bearberry leaves is a folk remedy for halting the spread of poison-ivy rash. The tannins in the leaves were once employed to dye leather and wool. The berries, however, are tasteless, except perhaps to bears and grouse.

Herbalists advise against long-term use of bearberry, as one of the active principles in the plant is toxic in large doses.

Belladonna

Atropa belladonna

Deadly nightshade, devil's berries

Habitat Native to Europe and South-west Asia; naturalized in eastern USA. Grows on wasteland, in quarries, ruins, and on wooded hills. Prefers shade, and chalk or limestone soils.
Description Perennial with stout, branched, purplish stem to 1.25m (5ft). All parts of the fresh plant smell unpleasant when bruised and are extremely poisonous. The stem divides higher up and bears dull-green, veined, oval leaves that are pointed at the apex and in pairs of unequal sizes. Dingy purple, furrowed, bell-shaped flowers tinged with green appear from mid to late summer, followed by shiny, black, juicy berries the size of a small cherry. **Parts used**: rootstock, leaves, berries.
History This exceptionally poisonous plant owes its botanical name to Atropos, one of the three Fates in Greek mythology who cut the thread of human life at the appointed time. Belladonna is probably in honour of the Italian ladies who made eye drops of the fresh juice to dilate their pupils and make them appear more alluring. In the Middle Ages belladonna was popular with witches who combined it with aconite in an ointment to produce the sensation of flying.

Belladonna's alkaloids, particularly atropine and hyoscyamine, are responsible for its powerful sedative and narcotic properties. Opthalmologists dilate the pupils with atropine, and it is an antidote to nerve gas. Belladonna extract is used medicinally to treat Parkinson's disease, whooping cough, and epilepsy. **CAUTION** All parts of the plant are highly poisonous.

Bergamot

Monarda didyma

Bee balm, Oswego tea, red bergamot

Habitat Native to North America on rich, moist soils from Maine, west to Michigan and Ontario, and south to Georgia. Naturalized in South America. Prefers part shade and grows wild in moist deciduous woods and thickets. Widely cultivated horticulturally as a border plant for its scarlet flowers.

Description Aromatic perennial with square, hairy, erect stem which grows up to 1m (3ft) tall. The leaves are fairly rough, oval and deep green. They are arranged in pairs and have serrated edges. In some cultivated varieties the leaves are mint-scented. From mid summer to early autumn very attractive tufted, scarlet flowers with two lips grow in whorls at the top of the stem. The whole plant smells pleasantly of orange. **Parts used**: leaves, flowers.

History Bergamot's common name, Oswego tea, reflects its popularity as a drink and also the area where it grew abundantly – the lands of the Otsego Indians in what is now New York. After the Boston Tea Party of 1773, bergamot became a popular substitute for expensive Indian tea.

In Native American medicine, bergamot is a traditional remedy for mild fevers, headaches, colds and sore throats. Some tribes also used the oil as a nasal decongestant. Today herbalists prescribe bergamot tea or syrup for nausea, flatulence, menstrual cramps, coughs and sore throats.

Growing tips Propagate from seed sown in spring or by root division. Seedlings take about a year to establish themselves and will grow well in ordinary garden soil, preferably light. Choose a sunny position for the plants, but with some shade.

Bethroot

Trillium erectum

Brown Beth, squawroot, stinking Benjamin

Habitat Native to North America from Quebec to North Carolina. This plant is found wild in shady, damp woods on rich, moist soils.

Description Perennial to 50cm (20in) with a short, thick root, rust-coloured externally and pale yellow inside. The broad, veined, stalkless leaves are almost square and taper to a point. They are grouped in threes in whorls at the end of the stem. In late spring, a small nodding, three-petalled white to brownish purple flower appears at the stem tip. **Parts used**: root and rhizome.

History Bethroot is a traditional Appalachian Indian remedy for treating disorders of the female reproductive system, hence the common name squawroot. The bethroot genus contains around 30 species but Native Americans considered this species the most effective medicinally and it was introduced into European medicine around 1830. Native Americans and Shakers valued the astringent properties of the dried root for stemming the flow of blood in post-partum haemorrhage, and used it to treat excessive menstrual flow. Modern analysis confirms the presence of steroid-like principles that act in a similar way to human sex hormones, and herbalists attribute the success of bethroot in treating menstrual disorders to these constituents. These steroidal substances also explain why Native Americans considered bethroot an aphrodisiac. The boiled roots were once employed to treat dysentery and diarrhoea.

Betony

LABIATAE

Stachys officinalis, Betonica officinalis

Wood betony, bishopswort

Habitat European native widely distributed in the UK but rare in Scotland. Found on light, sandy soils in open woodland, along wooded paths, in copses and meadowland.
Description Nettle-like perennial to 50cm (20in) with a square, grooved stem and a rosette of long-stalked, large basal leaves. The roughish upper leaves are stalkless, dotted with glands, and the margins have rounded teeth. From mid-summer to mid-autumn terminal spikes of two-lipped purplish-red flowers appear. **Part used**: flowering plant.
History This traditional remedy for headaches was once considered a cure-all that would drive away evil spirits.

Bistort

POLYGONACEAE

Polygonum bistorta

Snake root, easter ledge

Habitat European native and widespread in the north of England. May be found west of the Rockies in North America. Grows on roadsides, in damp meadows, open woodland, and on stream banks.
Description Perennial with a thick, black, twisted S-shaped root up to 1m (3ft) in length. Erect stem with swollen joints to 50cm (20in), with a few broad, dock-like leaves that taper to a point. The leaf stalks are crimson towards the base. Dense, conspicuous spikes of rose-pink or flesh-coloured flowers bloom from mid-summer to mid-autumn.
Parts used: root and leaves.

Blackberry

Rubus fructicosus

Bramble

Habitat Native to Europe and found in the north-eastern and central USA. Common hedgerow plant and widespread on shrubland, thickets, and wood edges. Invasive in gardens and near habitation. Cultivated for its fruit.

Description Sprawling shrub with woody and densely prickled stems. The trailing, tenacious stems can extend to 5m (15ft) and can easily root when in contact with the ground. The dark green leaves are grouped in threes or fives and are covered with fine hairs; the edges are serrated. White or pale pink flowers appear from mid-summer to mid-autumn followed by the familiar fleshy berries that ripen to black. Flowers and fruit may appear together on the same plant.

Parts used: fruit, leaves.

History In Europe, blackberries have been gathered from the wild for thousands of years. The juicy berries are traditionally made into jelly, pies, wine and vinegar, and from the late 17th century sweetened blackberry juice, plus spices and brandy, was considered an excellent cordial. In England, there are old country superstitions about the correct time for picking blackberries. According to legend, the devil fell from heaven on to a blackberry bush, and any blackberries picked after Michaelmas (29 September) will have the devil's spittle upon them.

Blackberry-leaf tea is a domestic remedy for sore throats and diarrhoea, while chewing the fresh leaves is an ancient cure for bleeding gums. The fresh, lightly boiled leaves were applied to piles, and blackberry vinegar is a home remedy of long standing for feverish colds.

Black Root

Veronicastrum virginicum

Culver's root, bowman's root

Habitat Native to North America, from New England to Kansas. Prefers moist woods and meadows, marshes and river banks.
Description Perennial to 2m (6ft) on a horizontal, blackish cylindrical rhizome. The stem is smooth, erect and unbranched and bears, at intervals, whorls of three to five lance-shaped leaves. Branching, terminal spikes of numerous white flowers appear from mid-summer to mid-autumn, followed by oblong seed capsules. **Parts used**: rhizome and root. **History** In Native American medicine, fresh blackroot was employed as a purgative, both medicinally and ritually.

Bladderwrack

FUCACEAE

Fucus vesiculosus

Kelp, sea-wrack

Habitat Commonly found on the coastlines of western Scotland, Norway, and the Atlantic coast of North America.
Description Strong-smelling, fan-shaped seaweed with a thin, leathery texture. The perennial frond is yellow to brownish green in colour and 1m (3ft) long. The stalk has a prominent mid-rib with pairs of air sacs running along its length. At the wavy tips, where the frond divides, are spherical receptacles filled with transparent mucous. **Parts used**: whole, dried plant.
History This common seaweed, the original source of iodine, is a herbal remedy for rheumatism.

Blessed Thistle

Cnicus benedictus

Sacred thistle, St Benedict thistle

Habitat Mediterranean native. Introduced throughout Europe and occasionally found wild in North America. Generally found in waste places on stony ground.

Description Annual, thistle-like plant with bristly, branched stems to 70cm (27in) that may bend under the weight of leaves and flower heads. The long, narrow, lance-shaped leaves are dark green with distinctive white veins. The margins are wavy with irregular indentations that end in sharp prickles. From early summer to early autumn pale yellow flowers appear, set in prickly green heads and partially concealed by brown spines. The whole plant is covered in down. **Part used**: flowering plant.

History Blessed thistle has been valued for its medicinal properties since the 16th century. It was once considered a cure-all and, together with another holy plant, angelica, was thought to offer protection against infection during the Great Plague. Sixteenth-century herbalists considered the herb a heart tonic and Shakespeare extols its medicinal virtues in *Much Ado About Nothing.* Culpeper prescribed blessed thistle for 'swimmings and giddiness in the head'. The leaves induce perspiration and act as a diuretic, and the herb is said to stimulate the flow of milk in nursing mothers. Modern herbalists value blessed thistle's bitter properties and consider it an effective appetite stimulant and a digestive tonic. In concentrated infusion, however, the herb is strongly emetic.

Blessed thistle once served as a vegetable: the root was eaten boiled and the head cooked like artichokes.

Blood Root

PAPAVERACEAE

Sanguinaria canadensis

Indian paint, red pucoon

Habitat Native to North
America and common in New
England. Grows on moist,
rich soils in woods and
on shaded slopes.
Description Perennial plant from
15–30cm (6–12in) on a thick rhizome
with orange-red rootlets that sends
up a sheathed leaf stalk. The leaf is
deeply lobed, hand-shaped, and
pale grey-green with toothed edges.
From mid-spring to early summer
a single, white, cup-shaped flower
with golden stamens appears. **Part used**: rhizome.
History The root yields a red juice that was used by Native
Americans as a body paint and fabric dye.

Blue Cohosh

BERBERIDACEAE

Caulophyllum thalictroides

Papoose root, blue ginseng

Habitat Native to eastern
North America, westwards
to Manitoba and southwards
to Tennessee. Found in
moist woodland.
Description Erect perennial
to 1m (3ft) with a knotted,
fragrant rootstock. The
mature, bluish-green oval leaves are
large, stalkless and usually divided
into three lobes. Yellow-green to
purplish-brown flowers with six petals
appear from late spring, followed by dark
blue pea-sized berries. **Part used**: root.
History Native American women drank blue cohosh tea
during the final stages of pregnancy.

Blue Flag

IRIDACEAE

Iris versicolor

Flag lily, liver lily

Habitat Native to central and eastern areas of North America, and introduced to Europe. Grows abundantly in swamps and bogs and prefers a peaty soil.
Description Perennial iris growing to 1m (40in) from a thick, creeping, dark brown rhizome. The thick, coarse stem bears long, sword-shaped, pale green leaves and in early summer purple-blue or violet flowers typical of the iris family appear. There are white or white and yellow markings at the base of each petal, and the flowers are succeeded by leathery seed ponds. **Part used**: rhizome.
History Liver lily, blue flag's common name, reflects its use in Native American medicine for liver and gastric ailments.

Bogbean

MENYANTHACEAE

Menyanthes trifoliata

Buckbean, marsh trefoil

Habitat Native to the northern hemisphere from the Pacific coast of North America, across Europe and Asia to Siberia. Grows in fresh-water marshes, bogs, and ditches, on peaty soils.
Description Perennial water plant with a dense matting of roots. The thick stem to 25cm (10in) is partly enveloped by the large, sheathing bases of the dark green leaves. These have a prominent pale midrib and three discrete, rounded lobes. From early summer distinctive, pinkish, five-petalled flowers covered with feathery white hairs appear.
Part used: leaves.
History A tea of this plant's bitter leaves is traditionally recommended for indigestion and to stimulate the appetite.

Boneset

Eupatorium perfoliatum

Feverwort

Habitat Native to Mexico, West Indies, and naturalized in North America. Common in open marshland, swampy ground and along the banks of streams from Dakota south to Florida.
Description Perennial from 60cm–1.5cm (2–5ft) on a thick, hairy, cylindrical stem. Branching above, the stem bears many lance-shaped, sharply pointed leaves with finely serrated edges. The dark green leaves are rough above and downy with resinous glands beneath. Short, dense, flat-topped clusters of white flowers appear from late summer to mid-autumn. The whole plant is slightly aromatic. **Parts used**: aerial parts.
History A Native American remedy for feverish conditions, boneset rapidly became popular among North American settlers. The name was coined following the herb's success in alleviating virulent strains of influenza, popularly called 'break-bone fevers'. Boneset's reputation spread to Europe and during the 18th and 19th centuries, it was the principal remedy for influenza and generally regarded as a panacea. Soldiers fighting in the Civil War were reputedly supplied with the herb to keep them free from infection and as a fever cure. Boneset tea was taken hot for a wide range of ailments from indigestion to malaria and typhoid.

Today, boneset is still employed medicinally to provoke beneficial sweating in cases of feverish colds, and small doses are a digestive tonic. Some herbalists regard boneset as highly overrated but research in India in 1975 suggested that the plant had potential for treating cancer.

Borage

Borago officinalis

Herb of gladness, burrage

Habitat Native to the Mediterannean region and naturalized throughout Europe and Britain. Cultivated commercially. Rarely found wild, except as an escape near habitation and on rubbish dumps.

Description Hardy annual, sometimes biennial, with erect stems to 60cm (2ft). The whole plant is covered with rough white hairs and is very prickly to the touch. The stem bears large, alternate, deep green leaves without stalks. They are oval in shape, veined, wrinkled, and pointed at the apex. From early summer to early autumn, striking bright-blue star-shaped flowers with distinctive black anthers appear at the ends of the branched stems. The flowers are very attractive to bees. **Parts used**: leaves and flowers.

History Borage, or herb of gladness, acquired a reputation for uplifting the spirits and dispelling gloom and this is referred to in all the historical writings on the herb. According to Gerard 'the leaves and flowers of borage put in wine do make men and women glad and merry and drive away all sadness, dullness and melancholy'. Culpeper assigned the astrological rulership of borage to Jupiter, planet of expansiveness and generosity, and put it under Leo, the sign that rules the heart. Modern herbalists respect borage's traditional uses and some continue to recommend it for restoring lost vitality and flagging spirits, especially during convalescence.

Borage leaves taste and smell pleasantly of cucumber, and the attractive blue flowers are traditionally added to summer drinks.

Growing tips Borage is self-seeding and very prolific. Sow seed in late spring in ordinary well-drained soil. Thin out and transplant to a sunny position.

Broom

Sarothamus scoparius

Scotch broom, bisom

Habitat Native to Britain, common in central and southern Europe, northern Asia, and naturalized in North America. Grows abundantly on heathland, and on the edges of woods and in woodland clearings. Prefers dry, sandy, acid soils.
Description Deciduous shrub to 1.5m (5ft). Bears many slender, wand-like, sparsely leaved branches similar to those of gorse but without prickles. The lower leaves have stalks and three oblong leaflets; the upper leaves are smaller and stalkless. Both sets of leaves are alternate and hairy when young. From early spring to mid-summer dense sprays of very fragrant, brilliant yellow, pea-shaped flowers appear. They are succeeded by flattened seed pods that become black on ripening and explode with a cracking sound. **Parts used**: flowering tops.
History In Medieval Europe, broom was known as *Planta genista* and was adopted as a heraldic emblem by one of the Dukes of Brittany. *Planta genista* became Plantagenet, the family name of the Duke's descendants from King Henry II to Richard III of England. Today, the Plantagenet emblem can still be seen in the broom pod motif that decorates the robe of Richard II's statue in Westminster Abbey.

Broom is a versatile domestic plant. Broom twigs were tied in bundles for sweeping floors, while witches made broomsticks of them and put them to a quite different use. Broom buds were pickled and eaten like capers, and the bitter young green tops added to ale. Medicinally, young broom shoots are mildly diuretic and a folk remedy for fluid retention.

Burdock

Arctium lappa

Beggar's buttons, gypsy's rhubarb

Habitat Widespread in Britain, Europe, and northern USA. Grows on waste ground, along fences, and on roadsides.
Description Biennial with stout, dull-green hairy stem to 1m (3ft) on a long, grey-brown, vertical root. The large leaves are dock-like, with long reddish stalks and wavy margins. They are furrowed above, woolly beneath, and roughen with age. Small, red or purple flowers that resemble thistles are set in distinctive fruiting heads covered with hooked burrs, appearing from late summer. **Parts used**: root, stalk, seeds.
History Burdock's botanical name *Arctium* is derived from the Greek for bear, a reference to the plant's rough burrs. In European folk medicine, the plant is considered a valuable blood-cleanser, and it was a well-established remedy among Native American tribes, particularly the Cherokee and Chippewa. Herbalists still recommend the root for the treatment of skin disorders, from pimples to acne and psoriasis. Burdock seed is said to act beneficially on the kidneys and the urinary system, and some herbalists claim that an infusion of the seeds has a tonic effect on the skin and hair. Poultices of the fresh leaves were applied to bruises and swellings.

Burdock root has a sweetish taste and was traditionally eaten boiled or roasted. The young stems may be cooked like asparagus, stir fried, or made into a soup. In Japan burdock is still cultivated as a vegetable.

Caraway

Carum carvi

Caraway seed

Habitat Widespread over northern and central Europe, temperate Asia, and the Middle East. Naturalized in the northern and northwestern USA. In Britain, most wild caraway is an escape. Tolerates most soils and prefers waste ground. Grown on a commercial scale in Germany, Holland, and the USSR.

Description Biennial on a slender, white taproot with hollow, ridged stems to 80cm (32in). The whole plant is pleasantly aromatic and has finely cut feathery leaves, long-stalked near the base and sheathed near the top of the stem. From late spring umbels of small white to cream flowers appear followed in late summer or early autumn by pale, oblong fruits (seeds) that are slightly curved and have five prominent ribs. **Part used**: seed (ripe fruit).

History Caraway seed has been found in Mesolithic excavations that date back five thousand years, and the Bible mentions its cultivation. In the Middle Ages the root was boiled and eaten and the young, chopped leaves added to soups and salads. In Elizabethan England a caraway-seed cake was traditionally offered to farm labourers when they had finished sowing the wheat.

Caraway seed contains a volatile oil that has digestive properties and a tea is a traditional remedy for flatulent indigestion. Caraway was also made into digestive 'comfits'. Herbalists still recommend caraway seed or oil for dyspepsia and for colic in children.

Growing tips Caraway tolerates most conditions but prefers moist soil and some sun. Sow the seed in summer or when it is ripe. Caraway grows vigorously and is self-seeding.

Cascara Sagrada

RHAMNACEAE

Rhamnus purshiana

Buckthorn, sacred bark

Habitat Native North American tree occasionally found wild in mountainous areas of the Pacific North West.

Description Deciduous tree to 8m (25ft) with chestnut-coloured bark that may be covered with a grey-white lichen. The leaves are dark green, oval, and clustered at the ends of the branchlets. In spring, small greenish flowers grow in umbels, followed by pea-sized berries ripening from scarlet to black. **Part used**: dried stem bark.

History Native Americans used the bark of this tree as a laxative and for digestive upsets. The effectiveness of the bark led early Spanish colonists to christen it *Cascara sagrada* – Spanish for sacred bark. Casacara sagrada's reputation soon spread over the USA and in the 19th century it became the foremost herbal remedy for chronic constipation. Extract of the bark was sold as a proprietary laxative in the late 19th century, and the bark was exported to Europe. Today, extract of the bark is still used in laxatives but herbalists prefer the dried bark, which tones the intestinal muscles. Most herbal laxatives contain matured bark since the fresh bark induces nausea and severe griping pains. Cascara is also thought to be effective when administered to dogs.

The plant's specific name *purshiana* is in honour of a 19th-century chemist called Pursh, who identified its active principles.

Catnip

Nepeta cataria

Catmint

Habitat Native to Europe and temperate Asia. Introduced in North America and other temperate zones. Widespread in central and southern parts of Britain. Grows on waste ground, field edges, railway banks, roadsides, and in hedgerows. Prefers chalky or gravelly soil.

Description Mint-like perennial with a strong, rather disagreeable smell on hairy, branched stems from 30–100cm (1–3ft). The silvery-grey leaves are coarsely toothed, heart-shaped, and downy on the underside. From late spring to late summer, dense whorls of white two-lipped flowers appear towards the top of the stems. The upper lip is spotted with dark crimson to violet, and the anthers are deep red to purple. Bees are attracted to the flowers. **Parts used**: flowering plant.

History When bruised or cut, the scent of catmint has an aphrodisiac effect on cats who have a tendency to roll in the plant and flatten it to the ground. Catmint-stuffed toy mice from pet stores hold a similar fascination for cats. According to folk wisdom, cats will not destroy catmint that has been grown from seed – 'if you sow it, the cats won't know it'. The scent has no demonstrable aphrodisiacal effect on humans.

Catmint tea is a traditional remedy for children's stomach upsets, and herbalists also recommend it for children's colic and diarrhoea. Catmint leaves were once smoked to relieve bronchitis and the plant acquired a dubious reputation as a narcotic.

Growing tips Sow seed in spring in rich soil in a situation with some shade, or propagate from cuttings taken in summer. Catmint is easy to grow and requires less watering than mint.

Cayenne

SOLANACEAE

Capsicum frutescens

Tabasco pepper, African pepper

Habitat Found wild in some tropical countries, notably
South America (Brazil) and South India. Supplies are said to
have come originally from French Guiana. Now cultivated in
South America, Africa, Asia and other tropical and sub-
tropical countries. May be grown successfully in warmer,
temperate climates.

Description Shrubby perennial plant from 30–90cm (1–3ft)
with a woody trunk when mature, and angular, purple-tinged
branches. The veined, stalked, leaves take various forms but
are usually elliptical and taper to a point. From early spring to
early autumn, drooping white or yellowish flowers hang in
twos or threes from long stalks. They are followed by small,
brilliant oblong pods that ripen to red or orange. These
'peppers' have an aromatic smell and contain many flat seeds.

Part used: ripe, dried fruit.

History Cayenne pepper took its name from Cayenne in
French Guiana where supplies originated. It is a close relative
of the sweet red bell pepper and the chilli
pepper, *Capsicum annuum*, and
bought cayenne may also
contain some of each
type. Cayenne is less
fiery than some
varieties of chilli and is widely
used in European, Creole,
Cajun, Mexican and East
Asian cuisines. It is the
principal ingredient
of hot tabasco sauce,
hence its name Tabasco pepper.

Cayenne is the preferred
species of *Capsicum* for
medicinal use. It acts as a
stimulant, an antiseptic,
and a digestive. Externally,
cayenne makes an excellent
liniment for poor circulation,
unbroken chilblains, sprains
and painful joints. Internally, small
doses of cayenne stimulate the
appetite and act as an internal cleanser.

Celandine, Lesser

Ranunculus ficaria

Pilewort

Habitat Native to Europe, western Asia, and North Africa. Widespread in moist meadows, ditches and hedgerows.

Description Familiar buttercup-like perennial with smooth, dark green, very glossy leaves that are sheathed at the base and heart-shaped. From early spring, solitary, star-like, bright yellow flowers are borne on long stalks. The flowers have between eight and ten petals, whereas the buttercup has only five. The flowers close before rain or in dull weather and become bleached with age. The plant is not related to the greater celandine *Chelidonium majus*. **Parts used**: whole fresh herb, including root.

History Celandine takes its specific botanical name from the Latin for fig, *Ficus,* since the many swollen tubers of the root resemble clusters of figs. To adherents of the Doctrine of Signatures, however, the bunched tubers resembled piles. On account of its success in treating this ailment, the plant became known as pilewort, and even today herbalists recommend a celandine ointment or a poultice for external application to haemorrhoids. The acrid juice from the tubers was once applied to warts.

All species of the genus *Ranunculus* – meaning little frog, after their preferred aquatic habitat – can irritate the skin. Herbalists advise against taking lesser celandine internally.

Celery, Wild

Apium graveolens

Smallage

Habitat Native to southern Europe. Found wild throughout Europe, Africa, North and South America, along tidal rivers and marshy ground near the sea.

Description Strong-smelling biennial with a bulbous fleshy root and coarse, ridged and branched stems from 30–60cm (1–2ft). The yellow-green to dark green leaves are opposite dentate, and very similar to those of garden celery. Throughout the summer sparse umbels of greenish-white flowers appear, followed by small, oval fruit (seeds). **Parts used**: fresh plant, seeds.

History Wild celery has a pungent smell and tastes bitter in comparison with cultivated celery, which was not introduced from Italy until the 17th century. The stalks of wild celery are greener, stringier, and much less swollen than the garden variety. Celery was popular with the Romans and widely used in Medieval cooking but today, many people find its smell overpowering. One recommendation is to dry the leaves in a spare room for a few weeks, then use to season soups.

Celery was first used medicinally to ease rheumatic pains, gout and arthritis. The fresh juice and the volatile oil in the seeds have a strong diuretic action, while the seeds, like many others in the Umbelliferae family, have a calming effect on the digestive system. Today, celery seed preparations are sold in health food stores for the relief of rheumatic aches and pains.

Centaury

Centaurium erythraea/Erythraea centaurium

Common centaury, European centaury

Habitat Central European native, widespread from western Europe to western Siberia. Introduced elsewhere. Found in dry, grassy places, roadsides and chalky slopes.

Description Annual with erect, square stem from 15cm–30cm (6in–12in) that branches near the top. The leaves at the base of the stem form a rosette; the stem leaves are smaller, pale green, lance-shaped, and arranged in pairs at intervals. From late summer to mid-autumn the stem is crowned with clusters of attractive rosy pink, star-like flowers with yellow stamens. **Parts used:** flowering herb.

History Centaury is named after the famous centaur of Greek myth, Chiron, who discovered the medicinal use of plants. Some herbalists recommend centaury for its strengthening effect on the arteries and capillaries. Large doses cause severe stomach irritation. During the Middle Ages magical powers were attributed to centaury, when people believed that it would repel evil spirits. Centaury blossoms are carved on the tomb of the famous English poet, Wordsworth. For him, the flowers, which open only in fine weather, resembled the rising sun.

Bitterwort was an old English name for centaury and its extreme bitterness, like that of the other members of the gentian family, has a tonic effect on the digestive system via a beneficial action on the liver and gall bladder. Taken before meals, centaury stimulates a flagging appetite. It is one of the bitter herbs added to aperitifs to encourage the appetite or act on a sluggish liver.

Chamomile, German COMPOSITAE

Matricaria chamomilla or *Matricaria recutita*

Wild chamomile

Habitat Native to Europe and northern Asia. Introduced in
North America. Widespread in meadows, along roadsides, and
on waste ground. Prefers light but moist soil. Cultivated
commercially in Central Europe, particularly Germany.

Description Sweet, delicately scented annual of the daisy
family with smooth, branching stems to 60cm (2ft). The
bright green leaves are deeply incised into thread-like
segments and have no stalks. Single daisy-like flowers appear
on long stalks from early summer to mid-autumn. The
blossoms may be distinguished from the garden chamomiles
by their yellow centres that are markedly conical and hollow.

Parts used: flowerheads.

History German chamomile is the preferred species of both
medical herbalists and homeopaths. *Matricaria* is derived from
either the Latin for mother, or from matrix, meaning womb.
Both derivations point to chamomile's traditional use for
female complaints including period pains, sore nipples and
thrush. The blue volatile oil in chamomile flowers is responsible

for its antispasmodic, antiseptic and anti-inflammatory action. Taken after a meal, chamomile tea is an excellent digestive, particularly for an upset stomach or heartburn, while in the evening, many find it a relaxing and sleep-inducing drink. A chamomile infusion, or the diluted essential oil, eases tension headaches and anxiety, and the herb also has a calming effect on restless children. In homeopathic dosage, chamomile is considered particularly appropriate for children's ailments such as teething, earache and colic. Externally, chamomile speeds up the healing of ulcers and burns, as well as skin problems such as eczema.

Growing tips Sow seed in early autumn for best results. Choose light but moist soil and a sunny position.

Chamomile, Roman COMPOSITAE

Chamaemelum nobile

Garden chamomile

Habitat Widespread over Europe and southern England on rough, dry pastures with sandy soil. Grown commercially in Central Europe and cultivated horticulturally.

Description Apple-scented, low-growing perennial to 30cm (12in) with trailing, branched and hairy stems. The leaves, like German chamomile, are deeply incised and finely feathery, but greyer-green and rather downy. The daisy-like flowers with yellow conical centres appear from mid-summer to mid-autumn on erect stalks. This variety has a much stronger fragrance than German chamomile. **Part used**: flower heads.

History Garden chamomile's distinctive apple scent made it a popular domestic strewing herb during the Middle Ages. In England, fragrant chamomile lawns were once popular: the herb gives off its sweet smell when trodden underfoot, and suffers no lasting damage.

Chamomile possesses similar properties to German chamomile and is popularly taken as a tea, made either from fresh or dried flowers. Chamomile-flavoured ale was once popular and chamomile flowers gave *manzanilla*, a Spanish sherry, its delicate flavour. Chamomile is widely employed as a cosmetic: an infusion of the flowers is an excellent, non-chemical lightener for fair hair, and makes a gentle skin tonic for sensitive skins. Chamomile flowers or oil may also be added to the bathwater for a relaxing effect.

Growing tips Sow in dry, sandy soil in spring, or, for double flower heads, propagate from offshoots in spring. Likes sun.

Chervil

Anthriscus cerefolium

Garden chervil

Habitat Native to the Middle East, south east Europe, and Asia. Naturalized in North America and cultivated in temperate and warm climates, especially France. Prefers light, well-drained soils.

Description Aromatic annual to 45cm (18in) with slightly hairy, fine grooved, branching stems. The delicate leaves, similar to those of cow parsley, are pale green, deeply divided, and fern-like. Lacy white flowers appear in flat umbels from late spring to mid-summer. **Part used**: leaves.

History Garden chervil is a graceful, sweet-smelling herb with a subtle, sweetish, anise-like flavour. It was introduced to Britain by the Romans but in culinary terms it has always been less popular both in Britain and the USA than in Europe. In French cookery, chervil is used extensively and considered interchangeable with parsley for flavouring and garnishing. Chervil is included in the classic *fines herbes* flavouring for omelettes, *bearnaise* sauce, and is commonly added to vinaigrettes. The herb must, however, be used fresh as its delicate flavour is lost on drying and with long cooking.

Chervil was once considered a cleansing, spring herb that made a welcome change after a heavy winter diet with few, if any, fresh green vegetables. Chervil stimulates the appetite and aids digestion while its mild diuretic qualities help to cleanse the system.

Growing tips Sow seed in late summer in light, well-drained soil. The plant needs warmth and shelter in the winter and some shade and moisture in summer.

Chickweed

Stellaria media

Starweed

Habitat Native to Europe but widely distributed all over the world. Naturalized in North America and Australia. A common weed on cultivated land and wasteland.

Description Ubiquitous annual with branched, straggling stems from 10–40cm (4–6in) that trail along the ground. The small, pale green leaves are oval with long stalks, and succulent like the stems. From early spring to late autumn numerous small, white five-petalled flowers appear that resemble stars. **Parts used**: aerial parts.

History As the common name and the French name *herbe à oiseau* suggest, chickweed has a long association with birds. It was traditionally fed to poultry and caged birds, and the fresh seed is a valuable source of food for small wild birds, particularly as it is available for most of the year. The young green stems have a taste reminiscent of spinach and country people fried them in butter or added them to salads.

Fresh chickweed has cooling and demulcent properties and was traditionally made into an ointment and applied to inflammations, swellings and haemorrhoids. According to Culpeper, who assigned the herb to the rulership of the Moon, chickweed 'doth wonderfully temper the heat of the liver, and is effectual for all impostumes and swellings whatsoever'. A chickweed poultice is a traditional home remedy for drawing out infection from boils and abcesses. Chickweed water acquired a reputation as a slimming aid, and some herbalists consider that the herb has a strengthening effect on the lymphatic and glandular systems.

Chicory

Cichorium intybus

Wild succory

Habitat Native to Europe and naturalized in North America, this plant is common on roadsides, waste ground, and field edges on light, sandy soil.

Description Perennial to 1.2m (4ft) on a large tap root. The bristly stem bears stiff, green, twig-like branches that are almost leafless towards the top. The jagged lower leaves are rough with hairs underneath. Large, sky-blue, dandelion-shaped flowers blossom from late summer to mid-autumn, closing up towards noon. **Parts used**: root and leaves.

History Chicory was cultivated in ancient Egypt and it was used medicinally from at least the first century. During the 16th and 17th centuries, when the Doctrine of Signatures prevailed, the milky juice of the root was taken as a sure sign that the plant would be beneficial for the sore breasts of nursing mothers. The bright blue flowers, on the other hand, symbolized blue eyes and a wash of the herb was recommended for eye inflammations. Chicory's medicinal virtues were certainly familiar to Queen Elizabeth I: she took chicory soup for its health-giving properties. Today, herbalists consider chicory a cleansing diuretic that acts as a liver tonic.

The ancient Egyptians and Arabs ate chicory leaves, and the roasted, ground root has been used both to flavour and adulterate coffee since the early 19th century. The young leaves, like those of the dandelion, are eaten in salads, while the forced leaves of cultivated varieties are a popular winter vegetable.

Chives

Allium schoenoprasum

Habitat Native to temperate and northern Europe.
Introduced and naturalized in North America. Occasionally
found wild on rocky, limestone soils but also grows on stream
banks and damp grassland. Cultivated widely both
commercially and horticulturally throughout northern Europe
and North America.

Description Hardy perennial and smallest member of the
onion family, growing to a height of 25–30cm (10–20in). The
hollow, grass-like, tubular leaves grow in clumps from small
flattish bulbs. In summer the flowering stem produces a
spherical head of numerous pale mauve flowers. These
conceal seed vessels containing small black seeds.

Part used: leaves.

History Chives are thought to have been used in Chinese
cooking as early as 3000 BC, but they were not cultivated in
Europe until the Middle Ages. Chives are known as the 'Infant
Onion' on account of the small bulb, and their mild flavour
may even be tolerated by those who either dislike
onions or find them difficult to digest.

In the kitchen, chives are
indispensable for flavouring a wide
variety of dishes, including soft
cheeses, sauces, vegetables,
omelettes and salads.
Chives lose their flavour
once they have been dried, but
can be kept for two or three
weeks in a plastic bag in the
fridge, or quick frozen.

Growing tips Chives are
easily grown either in the
garden or in pots indoors.
They will tolerate most
ordinary garden soils but
prefer a medium loam
and a semi-shaded
position. Sow seed in spring
or propagate by dividing clumps
in spring or autumn. Snip off the
flowering stems to encourage leaf
growth.

Cinquefoil

ROSACEAE

Potentilla reptans or *Potentilla canadensis*

Five-finger grass, five-leaf grass

Habitat European native
(*reptans*) and North
American native
(*canadensis*). Introduced
elsewhere. Common on
waste ground, hedgerows,
and grassy places.
Description Creeping
perennial on branched rootstock
with thread-like stems to 1m (3ft).
The leaves are divided into five,
sparsely hairy leaflets with
serrated edges and prominent veins on
the undersides. Yellow flowers, like those of the silverweed,
bloom from early summer. **Parts used**: leaves, root.
History During the Middle Ages, cinquefoil was commonly
included in love potions. Medicinally, it is an astringent.

Cleavers

RUBIACEAE

Galium aparine

Goosegrass, grip grass, sticky Willie

Habitat European native and
naturalized in North America. A
common weed of hedgerows,
roadsides, and field edges.
Description Annual with trailing,
straggling stems to 120cm (4ft) and
narrow, lance-shaped leaves in whorls
of six. Both stem and leaves are covered
with rough, hooked bristles.
Star-shaped, greenish-white
flowers appear in summer
followed by small, round seed
balls covered, like the stems, with the
hooked bristles. **Parts used**: flowering plant and fresh juice.
History Cleavers is a cleansing diuretic that helps to clear up
skin complaints.

Coltsfoot

Tussilago farfara

Son-before-father, coughwort, horse's hoof

Habitat Native to Europe, northern and western Asia, and North Africa. Introduced and naturalized in North America, from Nova Scotia southwards to West Virginia. Grows abundantly on waste ground, railway embankments, and on hard, bare, shingly ground.

Description Perennial to 25cm (9in) on spreading, white root with creeping, horizontal stems. The jagged, dandelion-like leaves on long stalks are covered with white, felted hairs when young. From early spring and before the leaves appear, single daisy-type yellow flowers appear at the ends of scaly, purplish stems. These are followed by seeds covered with tufts of silky, white hairs. **Parts used**: flowers and leaves.

History Coltsfoot and horse's hoof refer to the hoof-like shape of the leaves, while son-before-father reflects the plant's habit of flowering before the leaves appear. The botanical name *Tussilago* is a latin word meaning 'cough relieving', and coltsfoot, on account of its expectorant properties and soothing action, is a traditional remedy of long standing for coughs. The leaves were commonly smoked, and coltsfoot tea and coltsfoot syrup were standard domestic remedies for coughs, bronchitis and asthma. Coltsfoot was also made into a medicinal candy, known as coltsfoot rock. In Paris, coltsfoot was held in such esteem, that a flower painted on a door was the sign of a pharmacy.

CAUTION There is some controversy about the safety of coltsfoot, so it is advisable to use it only under professional supervision.

Comfrey

Symphytum officinale

Knitbone, bruisewort

Habitat Native to Europe and temperate regions of Asia. Introduced and naturalized in the USA and elsewhere. Found in rich, wet soils along stream and river banks, in ditches, in damp meadowland.

Description Perennial to 1m (3ft) on thick, dark brown rootstock. The stout, hollow stem and the leaves are rough with hairs, like borage. The ovate lower leaves are very large, the upper leaves are smaller, narrower and taper to a point. From early summer to early autumn, clusters of drooping flowers grow down one side of short, curved stalks. The flowers are bell-shaped and range in colour from creamy yellow to mauve or pale pink. **Parts used**: root and leaves.

History *Symphytum*, comfrey's botanical name, is derived from a Greek word meaning to join, and for centuries comfrey has been widely employed to mend or knit together broken bones. Comfrey poultices are also a traditional home-remedy of long standing for sprains, bruises, and cuts, and the herb was commonly grown in cottage gardens. Comfrey not only promotes healing, but further speeds up the process by reducing inflammation. Culpeper attributed comfrey's wound-healing and bone-knitting qualities to the influence of Saturn, planetary ruler of the skin and the skeleton. Comfrey's remarkable healing powers have been attributed to its high content of allantoin, a substance that promotes the growth of tissue, bone, and cartilage.

Growing tips
Comfrey tolerates most conditions but for best results, sow the seed in spring to summer in a rich, moist soil in a sunny position. The leaves make excellent compost.

Coriander

Coriandrum sativum

Common parsley

Habitat Native to the Mediterranean region and the Middle East. Widespread in many temperate zones in dry soils. Occasionally found wild in Britain. Cultivated commercially in India, parts of South America, Morocco, and in South Carolina in the USA.

Description Hardy annual to 60cm (2ft). The slender, branched stem bears flat, parsley-like lower leaves and feathery, thread-like upper leaves. The leaves are aromatic when crushed. Small, flat umbels of pretty white to pale mauve flowers bloom from mid-summer to mid-autumn followed by round, green berries (known as seeds) that drop as soon as they ripen. **Parts used**: leaves, dried ripe seeds.

History Coriander has been used both as a flavouring and a medicine for over 3000 years. The name coriander is derived from the Greek for bug, since the scent of the plant was supposed to be reminiscent of bed bugs. Coriander has always been a favourite culinary herb in the East, and the fragrant, strongly aromatic leaves give a characteristic flavour to curries and chutneys. They are extensively used in Chinese and South-east Asian cookery, hence the common name Chinese parsley. Coriander, once popular in Elizabethan times, is now enjoying a revival, especially as a flavouring for soups and salads.

The dried, ripe seeds have a sweet, spicy taste and aid the digestion of food. They are a feature of Indian and Indonesian cuisines, and in Europe are used as a traditional pickling spice.

Growing tips Sow the seed in late spring or autumn in shallow rows. Germination may be slow. Coriander needs a dry light soil and a sunny, sheltered position.

Corn Silk

Zea mays

Maize, Indian corn

Habitat Native to South America and cultivated in many parts of the world from Africa, Australia and India to Europe.
Description Well-known cereal crop. The stout stems bear cobs – several rows of yellow corn seeds enveloped in thin outer leaves. The silk is the soft filaments or beard that hangs from the husk. **Parts used**: styles or 'silk' around the cob.
History Corn silk is a soothing diuretic, useful for urinary infections.

Couch Grass

Agropyron repens

Twitch grass, dog's grass

Habitat Widespread European native. Naturalized in North America, especially eastern USA. A troublesome weed and common on arable land, waste ground and sandy places.
Description Perennial grass with a creeping underground rootstock that extends to 120cm (4ft). The smooth, hollow stems have greenish-grey flat leaves with roughish upper surfaces. Dense two-rowed spikes of small purple flowers bloom from mid-summer to early autumn.
Part used: rhizome.
History This common weed is used to treat cystitis and prostate trouble.
Ailing dogs are said to eat the grass to make themselves sick.

Costmary

Chrysanthemum balsamita

Alecost, Bible-leaf

Habitat Native to southern Europe and western Asia. Naturalized and cultivated in North America and Europe.

Description Perennial to 1m (3ft) with wide, grey-green, ovate, sweet-smelling leaves that have serrated edges. Some leaves have two small lobes at the base. The yellow, button-like flowers resemble those of tansy and appear in loose clusters from late summer to early autumn. **Parts used**: leaves and flowers.

History Costmary's old name is Balsam herb, on account of its fragrant leaves. During the Middle Ages, costmary was commonly grown in cottage gardens and its aromatic, faintly minty leaves were a popular flavouring for home-brewed ale – a use reflected in the herb's common name, alecost. Bible-leaf, another country name, refers to a custom prevalent among early American settlers. They used the long leaves to mark their place in Bibles and prayer books, reviving themselves with the pleasant scent or even chewing a piece of leaf during lengthy sermons. Costmary was also used in sachets, pot pourris, and to scent bathwater.

Costmary has digestive properties and was once a favourite English culinary herb. The fresh leaves may be added to green salads, soups, and to stuffings for poultry.

Growing tips In cooler climates costmary may not produce any seed, so propagation is difficult and must be achieved by dividing existing plants in spring. Costmary tolerates most soils and prefers a sunny spot.

Cowslip

Primula veris

Key flower, herb Peter

Habitat Native to northern and central Europe. Once common on porous chalky soils in meadows and pasture. Now becoming scarce due to over picking and pesticides.

Description Perennial to 30cm (12in) resembling the primrose but with shorter, more rounded leaves covered in fine hairs. The leaves form a rosette that lies almost flat on the ground. The long, slender stem is topped with clusters of pretty, nodding, pale yellow flowers usually spotted with orange. **Parts used**: flower petals and root.

History Cowslip is thought to be a corruption of cowslop, a reference to the dry meadows grazed by cattle that are the plant's favoured habitat. Key flower refers to the resemblance of the flower formations to bunches of keys, and in Norse mythology the flower is sacred to Freya, the Key Maiden. Herb Peter is an allusion to the plant's legendary origin: it sprang up where an agitated St Peter dropped the keys to heaven.

Cowslip flowers, which contain an essential oil with soporific properties, are traditionally made into an excellent, mildly sedative wine. Cowslip tea is a home remedy for restlessness, nervous headaches, and insomnia. In *A Midsummer Night's Dream*, Shakespeare alludes to the cowslip's alleged power to banish freckles and wrinkles. Cowslip root is expectorant and was once used to treat bronchitis.

Growing tips Sow seed in autumn in light, chalky soil in a sunny, grassy spot.

Dandelion Compositae

Taraxacum officinale

Piss-a-bed

Habitat Native to Europe and Asia. Introduced in many countries including North America and Australia. Common on soils rich in nitrogen in any situation.

Description Common perennial on thick taproot to 30cm (12in). A basal rosette of hairless, dark green leaves with large, jagged teeth rises straight from the root. From the centre grows a purplish, hollow flower stalk containing a milky juice. The familiar yellow flowers bloom from late spring to mid-summer followed by the seed head or 'clock' – a round ball of wispy, plumed seeds that can travel up to 10km (6 miles) in the wind. **Parts used**: root, leaves.

History The dandelion acquired its name from a fancied resemblance between its jagged leaves and a lion's teeth (in French, *dents de lion*). In the 16th century, dandelion became known as *Herba urinaria* because of the strong diuretic action of the leaves, a property still clearly reflected in its country name, piss-a-bed (in French, *pissenlit*). Modern herbalists still recommend dandelion for water retention, while the root, which has a tonic effect on the liver and gallbladder, is prescribed for liver ailments. Dandelion is also an effective blood-cleanser that is considered helpful for certain skin diseases.

Young dandelion leaves taste rather like chicory and are traditionally eaten in salads. The flowers have been made into a potent wine, and the root, leaves and flowers brewed into a variety of tonic beers, such as dandelion and burdock. Dandelion roots, like chicory roots, are usually roasted to produce an excellent caffeine-free coffee substitute.

Dill

Anethum graveolens

Dill weed

Habitat Native to the Mediterranean and southern USSR. Found wild in the Mediterranean in cultivated fields. Naturalized in North America. Widely cultivated and popular in herb gardens.

Description Aromatic annual to 1m (3ft), resembling fennel in appearance but smaller. The stems are smooth and shiny and the leaves pale green and very feathery. In mid- to late summer, flat umbels of small yellow flowers appear; the petals are turned inwards. They are followed by large quantities of oval, flat fruits, popularly called seeds. **Parts used**: dried ripe fruit and leaves.

History Dill's use is recorded in the Bible and it was well-known to the ancient Greeks and Romans. The name dill is thought to be a corruption of an old Norse word meaning to lull. Dill seeds contain a volatile oil that calms and settles the stomach, and dill water was once very popular for treating griping and colic in babies and small children. 'Meeting House' seeds is an old name that reflects the custom of chewing dill seeds during long church services to calm rumbling stomachs.

Dill is an important culinary herb. The fresh green leaves have a sharp, slightly sweetish tang and in Scandinavian and Polish cookery they are used like parsley. Dill seeds have a caraway-like flavour and are always used in pickling gherkins and cucumbers.

Growing tips Dill is a hardy plant that germinates quickly from seed sown in spring. Choose a sunny, sheltered spot and water regularly in dry weather.

Dog's Mercury

Mercurialis perennis

Habitat European native, common in woods and shady ground. Also found wild in eastern USA.

Description Foetid-smelling perennial to 40cm (16in) with a round, grooved stem covered with short, stiff hairs. The roughish, dark green leaves are opposite and ovate with serrated edges. Each leaf has two small lobes at the base. Small greenish flowers grow from the leaf axils, and appear just before the leaves have fully opened, from early to late spring. **Parts used**: fresh plant.

History Dog's Mercury is a poisonous plant with an acrid juice. According to legend, the Roman god Mercury revealed the plant's medicinal virtues, and in classical times the herb was known as Mercury's Grass. The old herbalists credited dog's mercury with remarkable healing powers but by the 17th century it was considered too hazardous for internal use. Culpeper complained that other herbalists failed to caution their readers against eating the fresh plant or wrote in Latin, which few people understood.

Dog's mercury's poison was said to be destroyed by boiling. The juice was once employed to remove warts and poultices were applied to swellings, infected cuts, and sores. Dog's mercury lotion once served as an antiseptic and an eyewash for sore eyes. Today, dog's mercury is little used.

CAUTION The fresh plant is poisonous.

Dog Rose

Rosa canina

Briar rose

Habitat Native to Europe, North Africa and western Asia. Naturalized in North America. Common in hedgerows, thickets, and shrubland.

Description Climbing rose with very prickly stems that grows to 3m (10ft). The bright green leaves are oval, finely serrated and taper to a point. The delicate, sweet-scented flowers appear from mid- to late summer and vary in colour from white to palest pink. They are quickly followed by fruits, called hips, that ripen to deep red and become soft and fleshy.

Parts used: rose hips and leaves.

History Wild white roses were once very common in England and the wild rose is the country's national flower. In Latin *alba* means white and Pliny apparently thought that England's old name, Albion or Alban, reflected the abundance of wild roses. The plant's common and botanical names either allude to a medieval belief that the plant would cure rabid dog bites, or the prefix dog may be a corruption of dag or dagger – a reference to the plant's sharp prickles.

Rose leaves were once drunk as a tea substitute and they have a mild laxative effect. Culpeper recommended the fresh hips for consumption and chest infections, and the dried hips for urinary stones. Rose hips are rich in Vitamin C and are traditionally made into conserves and purées. They were collected from the wild during World War II when citrus fruit was scarce. Rosehip tea has a mild diuretic and tonic effect, and the fresh petals can be made into a delicate jam.

Dyer's Greenweed

LEGUMINOSAE

Genista tinctoria

Dyer's broom, greenwood

Habitat Native to the Mediterranean and western Asia. Naturalized in North America. Grows wild on heathland and rough pasture land.

Description Perennial broom-like shrub to 60cm (2ft) with erect, stiff branches bearing simple, alternate, spear-shaped leaves. From mid-summer to early autumn, bright yellow pea-flowers, similar to those of gorse and broom, grow in thick spikes at the end of the shoots. These are followed by smooth seed pods that ripen to brown and burst open. **Parts used**: flowering plant, seeds.

History For the Romans and the inhabitants of certain Greek islands, dyer's greenweed was a valuable dye plant. The flowering tops of dyer's greenweed yield a yellow dye and this was extensively used to colour wool, linen and leather. A green shade is produced when the flowers are combined with another ancient dye plant, woad.

The seeds of the fresh plant have a mild purgative effect and the flowering plant has diuretic properties. Dyer's greenweed was used medicinally to treat dropsy, and an ointment was a popular 14th-century remedy for gout and rheumatism. The seeds were apparently mixed with a type of plaster for setting broken limbs. Herbalists have discovered that dyer's greenweed can raise the blood pressure. Today, it is rarely used medicinally.

Echinacea Compositae

Echinacea angustifolia

Purple coneflower, Kansas snakeroot

Habitat Native to the North American prairies as far north as southern Canada. Found on grassland, in open woods, and on roadsides.

Description Perennial on thick, bristly stem to 45cm (18in) with ovate leaves that taper to a sharp point at both ends. From early summer to early autumn, faintly aromatic, solitary flowers appear on stout stalks. The purple centres are distinctly conical in shape and surrounded by dullish purple ray florets. **Part used**: rootstock.

History Echinacea was one of the most important herbs to Native Americans, who discovered the medicinal properties of the root. During the 1900s it was the foremost remedy amongst all the Plains Indian tribes for snakebites, venomous insect bites, and burns. Native Americans also employed the fresh juice of the herb to desensitize their feet before fire walking rituals over hot coals. They considered echinacea root an excellent blood cleanser for clearing up septic sores, boils, and abcesses.

Modern research has confirmed the root's antibacterial properties and herbalists believe that echinacea both strengthens and stimulates the immune system.

Growing tips Sow seed in ordinary, well-manured garden soil in late spring or early summer, when the soil is warm. Echinacea is a hardy plant that is easy to care for. It prefers a sunny position.

Elder

Sambucus nigra

Pipe tree, bour tree

Habitat Native to Europe, western Asia, and North Africa. Introduced and naturalized in North America. Common in hedgerows, copses, the edges of woods, and near dwellings.
Description Familiar, fast-growing shrub or small tree to 7m (24ft) with a cork-like bark. The dark green leaves are grouped in fives with finely serrated edges that taper to a point. In summer, tiny sweet-smelling, creamy-white flowers grow in flat-topped umbels, followed by drooping bunches of small, juicy, purple-black berries. **Parts used**: berries, flowers, bark and leaves.
History It was once customary for rural children to hollow out young elder stems and use them as blowpipes, hence the common name pipe tree. In English folklore, elder juice had magical properties and any baptized person, merely by smearing it around the eyes, could foresee the approach of a witch. In Scandinavian fairy tales, the Elder-tree mother lived in the tree and had to be consulted before branches could be cut down for wood.

The elder became known as the 'medicine chest of country people'. Elderberries were made into a warming winter cordial for chesty colds, while the flowers promote sweating and are an ingredient of 'composition essence', a traditional herbal cold cure. Elderflower water is an old-fashioned skin tonic. When outdoors, an infusion of bruised elder leaves will help to deter flying insects.

Elecampane

Inula helenium

Scabwort

Habitat Native to Central and southern Europe. Naturalized in North America, from Nova Scotia to North Carolina. Widespread on damp soils in shady hedgerows, along roadsides, and on waste ground. Prefers shady situations.

Description Tall, striking plant with stout, hairy stems to 1.5m (5ft) growing from a thick, brown, aromatic taproot. The large leaves, up to 30cm (12in) in length, are hairy above, downy beneath and pointed. The lower leaves have long stalks, the upper are stalkless. From early to late summer bright yellow, ragged, sunflower-like blossoms enclosed by downy bracts appear on long stalks. **Part used**: root.

History Elecampane, according to legend, is Helen of Troy's plant, which sprang from her tears when she was abducted by Paris. Culpeper assigned elecampane to Mercury's rulership – a planet associated via the sign of Gemini with the voice and lungs – and prescribed the herb for coughs and lung problems. Scientific analysis has shown that inulin, the root's active principle, is a powerful expectorant of fluid from the lungs, and herbalists still consider elecampane a most effective remedy for respiratory disorders.

In Elizabethan England, elecampane roots were sugared and eaten as a sweetmeat, while in Switzerland, the root extract was used as a flavouring for the liqueur, Absinthe.

Growing tips Propagate from root cuttings. Cover and store until spring, then plant out in moist, well-drained soil in a shady position.

Eucalyptus

Eucalyptus globulus

Tasmanian blue gum

Habitat Native to Tasmania and Australia. Introduced in Central and South America, in California, Africa, India, southern Europe, and Ireland.

Description Tall, attractive tree growing to 60m (195ft) or 35m (115ft) in cooler climates. The trunk is smooth and cream coloured with a covering of greyish-blue bark that peels off in narrow strips. The narrow, leathery, sword-shaped leaves have a prominent mid-rib. They are studded with oil glands, fragrant and greenish-blue colour. Creamy-white flowers are borne on short flat stalks, followed by fruit that is concealed in an aromatic, camphor-scented, woody cup.

Parts used: leaves and oil.

History The eucalyptus can store quantities of water in its roots, and for this reason, the tree was planted in swampy 'fever districts' to dry up the marshes and prevent outbreaks of malaria. Native Australian aborigines discovered the medicinal properties of eucalyptus oil, and it is still highly valued by both orthodox and herbal practitioners for its strongly germicidal, expectorant, and decongestant properties. Eucalyptus oil is commonly found in proprietary throat lozenges, while steam inhalations are particularly beneficial for clearing the head and chest of mucus and catarrh.

Eucalyptus plantations destined for paper pulp have provoked severe criticism from environmentalists as some virgin forests have been cut down to make way for this fast-growing, water-loving species.

CAUTION Unsafe in large doses.

Evening Primrose

ONAGRACEAE

Oenothera biennis

Evening star

Habitat Native to North America. Introduced and naturalized in Europe. Grows on dry, sandy and stony soil on wasteground, railway embankments, and sand dunes.
Description Biennial, occasionally annual, with a branched, reddish stem growing from 100–130cm (3–4ft). The alternate leaves are lance-shaped and rather hairy. From mid-summer attractive, pale lemon-yellow flowers bloom all along the stem and in a spike at the tip. Opening in the early evening, the flowers have four large petals and a subtle fragrance, and are followed by tubular, pointed seed pods. **Part used**: oil from seeds.
History The evening primrose acquired its name because of its pale yellow blossoms open in the evening. In recent years the plant has been extensively tested and analysed, due to the gamma linoleic acid (GLA) in the oil extracted from its seeds. GLA is a hormone-like substance that, according to the testimony of many sufferers, brings relief from such premenstrual discomforts as bloating, sore breasts, and mood swings. In Britain, evening primrose supplements and preparations for treating PMS are widely available at pharmacies and health food stores. Externally, evening primrose oil has been used successfully to treat eczema, psoriasis, dandruff, and dry, flaking skin. Current research is being directed at the effectiveness of the oil in treating multiple sclerosis.
Growing tips
Sow ripe seed in late summer. The plant prefers dry, sandy ground and a sunny position. It is self-seeding.

Eyebright

SCROPHULARIACEAE

Euphrasia officinalis

Meadow eyebright

Habitat Native European plant that is common throughout Britain in meadows, and on rough pastureland and heathland. Prefers chalky soils.

Description Small annual to 15cm (6in) with opposite, oval leaves that have scalloped edges. At the top of the stem, spikes of small, white flowers appear from mid-summer to late autumn. The flowers are variable but are usually lipped, veined with purple and flecked with yellow. They are followed by tiny capsules containing many ribbed seeds. **Parts used**: flowering plant.

History As the name suggests, eyebright is a traditional remedy for eye problems. In France the herb's popular name is *casse-lunettes*, loosely translated as 'throw away your glasses'. Eyebright was known to the ancient Greeks but its medicinal status was firmly established by subscribers to the Doctrine of Signatures. They likened the purple-veined white flowers with yellow spots to a bloodshot, diseased eye, and designated the plant a cure for eye problems. Eyebright juice was taken in white wine, as a tea, and even made into an ale. Today, eyebright has maintained its position as the foremost herbal eye medication, and herbalists recommend an eyebright wash where there is a discharge from the eyes, for conjunctivitis, and for allergic reactions that affect the eyes.

Growing tips Eyebright is difficult to grow as it is a semi-parasitic plant. It feeds off grass and other plants by attaching suckers to the roots and drawing out the nutrients it requires. It will not, however, permanently damage grass.

Fennel

Foeniculum vulgare

Wild fennel

Habitat Native to the Mediterranean. Introduced and naturalized in Europe and North America. Grows on sea cliffs, coast paths and waste ground. Prefers dry soils.

Description Hardy perennial that resembles dill but is taller and stouter, growing to 1.5m (5ft). The thick, blue-green stems bear aromatic, feathery, fan-shaped leaves with thread-like leaflets. From early summer to early autumn, flat umbels of mustard yellow flowers appear followed by brown fruits (seeds). **Part used**: seeds.

History Fennel's culinary use dates back at least 2000 years, and it is the wild ancestor of the bulbous Florence fennel that is so popular in Italian cookery. Wild fennel tastes bitter in comparison but the young green stems are said to be edible. Fennel is mentioned in Anglo-Saxon recipes and was traditionally eaten with salted fish during Lent. This combination fulfilled the dual function of checking flatulence and making the fish more digestible.

Medicinally, fennel seed has long been used to expel wind and is popularly taken in the form of a tea. After spiced Indian dishes, fennel seed is traditionally offered as a digestive and to sweeten the breath. In the 17th century fennel seed acquired a reputation as a slimming aid, and the seeds were commonly chewed to relieve hunger pangs.

Growing tips Sow the seeds in spring in a sunny position, preferably in a light, well-drained soil. Keep the soil moist after sowing but do not overwater.

Fenugreek

PAPILIONACEAE

Trigonella foenum-graecum

Bird's foot

Habitat Native to the Mediterranean and western Asia. Naturalized in North America. Widely cultivated in the Middle East, India, and North Africa.

Description Fragrant, erect annual to 50cm (20in) with a round, smooth stem. The leaves are grouped in threes, like clover leaves, but have toothed margins and hairy stalks. In mid-summer, white to yellowish pea-like flowers grow from the leaf axils. They are followed by narrow, beaked seed pods, often sickle-shaped, containing between ten and twenty brown seeds. **Part used**: seed.

History The ancient Greeks used fenugreek in cooking and it was introduced into European medicine before the 9th century by Benedictine monks. The aromatic seed has a slightly bitter celery-like taste and is a common flavouring in curries and chutneys. The young green leaf may also be curried. In the Middle East roasted fenugreek seed served as a coffee substitute, and it is ground with sesame seed to make the sweetmeat halva. The seeds are particularly nutritious when sprouted, like alfafa.

Fenugreek seed has acquired something of a reputation as an aphrodisiac, and chemical analysis has revealed the presence of diosgenin, a substance that acts in a similar fashion to the body's own sex hormones. Fenugreek is an old remedy for increasing the flow of milk in nursing mothers, and Chinese herbalists recommend it for impotence and for restoring hair growth to balding scalps.

Growing tips Fenugreek will thrive in rich, well-drained garden soil. Sow in spring in a sunny position. The seeds reach maturity in about four months and are then ready for drying.

Feverfew

Chrysanthemum parthenium or *Tanacetum parthenium*

Featherfew, featherfoil

Habitat Native of south-east Europe. Naturalized elsewhere including Britain and North America – from Ohio to Missouri and California. Found on wood edges, walls, hedgerows, roadsides, and waste ground. Cultivated commercially, and a double-flowered variety is grown horticulturally.

Description Perennial plant with branched, hairy stems to 50cm (20in) that are trailing in habit. The fan-shaped, yellow-green leaves have a strong, slightly bitter scent and are deeply lobed. The upper leaves toothed and segmented. From mid-summer to mid-autumn clusters of daisy-like flowers appear with flat, not conical, centres. **Part used**: leaves.

History Feverfew, a corruption of the Latin *febrifugia* or *febrifuge*, was once the foremost cure for 'ague' – a type of fever characterized by alternate bouts of shivering or burning. The fresh leaves were bound around the sufferer's wrists. The herb was also planted around cottages to keep out disease. Today, feverfew is no longer prescribed for fevers but has sustained its reputation as a home remedy for indigestion, sleeplessness and headaches. Feverfew has been subjected to clinical trials following claims that eating the fresh leaves cured migraine attacks. One study found that after taking feverfew one in three sufferers had no further attacks. Some herbalists recommend eating small amounts of feverfew daily as a preventive measure against migraines, but warn that some people may develop mouth ulcers.

Growing tips Sow the seeds in early spring, preferably indoors or under glass. Plant out in well-drained soil in a sunny, sheltered position.

Figwort

Scrophularia nodosa

Knotted figwort, scrofula plant

Habitat Native to Europe and introduced in North America from Maine to Kansas. Common in wet woodland, thickets, near streams and ditches, and in damp, shady places.
Description Strongly scented perennial to 90cm (3ft) on a tuberous rootstock. The stem is dull green, often purplish, with opposite pairs of heart-shaped leaves. From early summer to early autumn, spikes of greenish-brown flowers appear, followed by oval, pointed, seed capsules. **Parts used**: rootstock, flowering plant.
History Figwort's botanical name *Schrophularia*, and its common name, scrofula plant, point to its traditional use in the treatment of scrofula – a once prevalent tubercular disease characterized by glandular swellings. Figwort is thought to stimulate the lymphatic system and acts as an internal cleanser and diuretic. Cuts, septic sores, and inflammations were once treated with an ointment of the fresh plant, and it acquired a dubious reputation as a cure for hydrophobia – a dread of swallowing water symptomatic of rabies. Today, on account of its cleansing and mild purgative action, figwort is principally used in the treatment of skin problems.
CAUTION The herb is a mild heart stimulant and must be avoided by those with heart conditions.

Flax

Linum usitatissimum

Linseed

Habitat Origin uncertain. Widely distributed in temperate zones and cultivated commercially in northern Europe, the north-western USA, and the Soviet Union. Found wild only as an escape, on waste ground and roadsides.

Description Graceful, slender annual to 60cm (2ft) with erect stems branching from the base. The narrow, stalkless leaves are lance-shaped and marked with three veins. From early to late summer five-petalled, pale blue flowers appear, followed by a round pea-size capsule containing shiny brown seeds. **Parts used**: seeds, oil, fibre.

History Flax has been cultivated since 5000 BC for its valuable fibre: the specific botanical name *Usitatissimum*, meaning most useful, reflects the value and varied uses of flax. Early societies made clothing, rope, cord, fishing nets, and sails from the soaked and dried fibrous stems, and today flax is still extensively cultivated in Ireland, northern Europe and the USA for linen manufacture.

Linseed, the ripe seed of the flax plant, is the part used medicinally. Poultices of the crushed, ripe seed are traditionally made for drawing boils and inflammations, while linseed tea is a soothing and healing remedy for chest and lung infections. The seed also makes an effective bulk laxative. The light yellow oil obtained from flax seeds, known as linseed oil, was formerly taken to ease the passage of gallstones through the body but is no longer used medicinally.

Foxglove

Digitalis purpurea

Fairies' gloves, dead man's bells

Habitat Familiar western European wild flower, widespread in Britain and introduced in North America, especially in northern and central states. Common in hedgerows, wood edges, lanes, roadsides and dry meadows.

Description Biennial, sometimes perennial, from 120cm–2m (4–6ft) producing a long, stout, flowering stem in the second year. At the base is a rosette of large, downy, grey-green leaves with finely indented margins and stalks. The stem leaves are progressively smaller towards the top, and short-stalked. From early summer to mid-autumn the familiar bell-shaped drooping flowers appear. They are crimson to purplish-pink in colour, and mottled with white inside. **Part used**: leaves.

History The foxglove has an old association with the fairies or good folk, and the white markings inside the flowers are said to be elves' fingerprints. Fairies reputedly showed the fox how to muffle his footsteps with the flowers so that he could catch more farmyard chickens.

In 1785 William Withering found that foxglove leaves contained a substance that not only strengthened the heartbeat but encouraged the kidneys to eliminate excess fluid from the body. Foxglove tea was traditionally drunk in the English Midlands for dropsy – a disease characterized by fluid retention. Today, digitoxin, the main active principle, is employed in orthodox medicine as a heart stimulant.

CAUTION All parts are highly toxic. To be used only under medical supervision.

Fringe Tree

Chionanthus virginicus

Snowdrop tree, old man's beard

Habitat North American native found south to Texas and Florida, and also in New England. Grows in woods and along river banks on rich, moist soil. Cultivated as an ornamental.
Description Small deciduous tree to 8m (25ft) with smooth, oval leaves similar to those of the magnolia. From late spring when the leaves are not yet fully open, clusters of fragrant and delicate white flowers with fringe-like petals appear. They are followed by oval purple berries. **Part used**: root bark.
History The root bark of *Chionanthus*, from the Greek meaning snow flower, is a traditional liver remedy .

Fumitory

FUMARIACEAE

Fumaria officinalis

Earth smoke

Habitat Native to Europe and widely naturalized. Found on roadsides and a common weed in gardens.
Description Small, slender, densely spreading annual from 15–70cm (6–27in). The grey-green, segmented leaves are fan-shaped. From mid-summer to late autumn, spikes of small, pink, tubular flowers appear. Tipped with dark purple, or sometimes white, the upper petal is pouched at the base. **Parts used**: flowering plant.
History Fumitory, which was once burnt to drive out demons, has long been employed as a liver and skin tonic.

Garlic

LILIACEAE

Allium sativum

Habitat Thought to be native to Asia, and possibly southern Siberia. Cultivated in the Mediterranean region for centuries. Introduced to all warm climates.

Description Perennial or biennial member of the onion family with a bulb consisting of several cloves enveloped in a pinkish-white, parchment-like coating. The stem, from 15–30cm (6–12in), is unbranched and bears long, flat, pointed, grass-like leaves that are sheathed at the base. At the tip of the stem a rounded umbel of whitish flowers appears, often interspersed with small bulbs. Before flowering, the umbel is encased in a teardrop-like membrane that tapers to a sharp, green point. **Part used**: bulb.

History Garlic was so highly esteemed by the ancient Egyptians that the slaves building the Great Pyramid at Cheops were given a daily supply. To the ancient Greeks garlic was a magical, protective herb and they left offerings at crossroads to placate the underworld goddess Hecate.

Garlic has antibacterial properties that help the immune system to fight infection. Its antiseptic properties were invaluable in World Wars I and II, when it was used to stop wounds turning septic. It may be taken as a preventative against colds, and also coronary artery disease since it lowers blood cholesterol levels. In the Middle Ages, garlic was regarded as a vegetable and eaten with relish. Today, although it is used in cooking all over the world, we tend to use it with rather more restraint.

Growing tips Plant individual cloves in early spring to a depth of 5cm (2in) in rich, well-drained soil in a sunny, sheltered position. Lift when the tops have withered.

Gentian, Yellow GENTIANACEAE

Gentiana lutea

Habitat Native of Central European Alpine meadows. Widespread in mountainous regions of southern and eastern Europe. Cultivated commercially in eastern Europe and North America.

Description Perennial on a thick yellowish taproot to 30cm (12in). The stem reaches 110cm (43in) and at each joint bears a pair of veined, yellowish-green leaves oval in shape and tapering to a point. In late summer whorls of attractive bright yellow, star-shaped flowers appear in the leaf axils of the upper stem. **Part used**: root.

History Egyptian records show that gentian was used medicinally as early as 1200 BC. The ancient Greeks recommended gentian root for stomach and liver problems and it was thought to offer protection against infectious disease, possibly on account of its unremittingly bitter taste. Gentian's reputation as a guard against infection appears to have persisted into the Middle Ages when it was used to antidote poisons. Gentian root is indeed remarkable for its virtually unrivalled bitterness, and is considered a valuable digestive tonic. It works by stimulating the production of digestive juices and improves both appetite and digestion. Herbalists recommend gentian root for loss of appetite, dyspepsia and flatulence. The fermented and distilled root is still a common ingredient of bitter European aperitifs and liqueurs.

Growing tips Yellow gentian requires a deep loamy or peaty soil and a sunny position with shelter from cold winds. Sow the seeds in spring in a cold frame.

Ginger

Zingiber officinale

Habitat Probably native to South-east Asia, particularly China. Introduced and cultivated in many other tropical countries including Jamaica, West Africa, India, Australia, and the USA, in southern Florida. Requires shade, rich, well-drained soil, and a tropical climate.

Description Perennial on stout, buff-coloured, aromatic, tuberous rhizome with swollen finger-like joints. In spring the rhizome produces an erect, reed-like stem growing from 60–120cm (2–4ft) with narrow, sword-shaped leaves. The flowering stem produces spikes of fragrant yellowish-white or greenish-white lipped blossoms, streaked with purple. **Part used**: rhizome.

History Ginger found its way from the East to southern Europe long before the days of the Roman Empire. In the 16th century, the Spanish established ginger cultivation in Jamaica. At first Chinese crystallized ginger and the dried root, usually sold ready ground, were principally imported, but now the fresh root is widely available.

Ginger root has warming, aromatic properties and is a traditional home remedy for colds and flu.It promotes a beneficial sweating that helps to eliminate toxins from the system, and may be taken as a tea with honey and lemon at the first signs of a chill. The fresh or dried root also stimulates the circulation and is helpful for cold hands and feet. Ginger has a calming effect on the digestive system and one study found it was beneficial for travel sickness.

Growing tips Plant fresh root ginger in a pot and keep it in a warm, moist atmosphere, putting it outside in the shade during hot weather.

Ginseng, Oriental ARALIACEAE

Panax ginseng or *Panax pseudoginseng*

Chinese or Korean ginseng

Habitat Native to East Asia, particularly Manchuria in China, and also Korea. Once found wild in cool, damp woods but now extremely rare. Cultivated in China and Korea.

Description Perennial from 60–80cm (24–30in) on an aromatic, branched rootstock that is often forked. The single, erect stem is reddish and produces, near the top, a whorl of three to five ribbed leaves. These are oval in shape with finely serrated edges and taper to a point. From mid to late summer and after three to four years, sparse umbels of greenish-yellow flowers appear at the tip of the stem, followed by bright red berries. **Part used**: dried root.

History Ginseng takes its name from *renshen*, a Chinese word meaning man-root, after the curiously human-like root with its two legs. On account of its shape, Chinese herbalists pronounced ginseng a herb of well-being and it was extensively employed in Chinese medicine for centuries. Particularly fine specimens were valued more highly than gold. Ginseng seems to have acquired a reputation as a cure-all and many extravagant claims have been made for its powers, from improved memory function to longevity. It works by strengthening the whole body so that it can more easily deal with stress and infection, and it has no demonstrable effects on a healthy system. Modern herbalists advise that ginseng should be treated with respect and taken only in times of stress, as an occasional helper.

Ginseng, American

Panax quinquefolium

Five-fingers, five-leafed ginseng

Habitat Native to
cool, wooded areas of
eastern and central North
America, from Quebec and
Ontario south to
Oklahoma and
Alabama. Now thought
to be unknown in its wild state.
Cultivated commercially,
principally in Wisconsin.
Description Similar in
appearance to oriental
ginseng, but smaller, and
with pinkish-coloured flowers.
The leaves are more oblong in shape, tapering less, and more
abruptly pointed: the margins are coarsely serrated or toothed.
Part used: root.
History Native Americans used ginseng root medicinally, and
it was a common ingredient of love potions. American ginseng
is thought to be less potent than oriental ginseng.

Goldenrod

COMPOSITAE

Solidago virgaurea

Woundwort, European goldenrod

Habitat Native to Europe,
northern and western Asia. Grows
on heathland, grassland, dry banks
and cliffs.
Description Erect perennial to 1m
(3ft) with sparsely branched stems
and oval, pointed leaves with very
slightly toothed margins. From late
summer to autumn, spikes of daisy-
like golden flowers appear towards the
end of the stem. **Parts used**: flowering plant.
History This old wound-healing herb takes its botanical
name from the Latin verb meaning to strengthen.

Golden Seal

Hydrastis canadensis

Orange root, eye balm, yellow puckoon

Habitat Native to Canada and the eastern USA. Once found in shady woods and meadows with rich, moist, soil. Now becoming rare in the wild.

Description Low perennial from 15–30cm (6–12in) on a thick, twisted, horizontal rhizome that is brownish externally and bright yellow inside. In early spring two large, prominently-veined, five-lobed leaves appear at the top of the hairy, cylindrical stem. From late spring the plant produces a solitary greenish-white flower with numerous stamens but without petals, followed by a raspberry-like fruit. **Parts used**: root and rhizome.

History Golden seal is a celebrated Native American medicinal and dye plant. The Cherokee tribe stained their skin and clothes with the yellow juice from the root and used the powdered root to heal wounds, rashes, and watering eyes. It was also customary to chew the fresh root to relieve mouth ulcers. American settlers soon recognized golden seal's medicinal properties and the herb was widely regarded as a cure-all. It became popularly known as poor man's ginseng.

Today herbalists employ golden seal root for its tonic and healing effect on the digestive system, especially where there is inflammation. An infusion of the powdered root is still employed as a soothing, antiseptic eye lotion, and also serves as an astringent mouthwash for sore gums and throat infections.

CAUTION Golden seal may stimulate the uterus to contract. Avoid during pregnancy.

Gravelroot

Eupatorium purpureum

Queen of the meadow, Joe-pye weed

Habitat Native to North America. This distinctive plant grows in damp woodland and low, swampy meadows from southern Canada as far south as Florida.

Description Tall, striking plant from 1–3m (3–9ft) with a purple tinged, hollow stem bearing whorls of lance-shaped, roughish leaves with irregularly serrated edges. The leaves are downy beneath and have a vanilla-like scent. From late summer to mid-autumn clusters of attractive whitish flowers marked with purple appear. **Part used**: dried root.

History Gravelroot's botanical name *Eupatorium* refers to Mithridates Eupator, a celebrated herbalist of the first century BC, who may have been the first to use it medicinally. Native Americans used the plant to provoke sweating and, like its relative, boneset, considered it a fever cure. One tribe apparently considered the plant an aphrodisiac. Its popular name, Joe-pye weed, is in honour of an American Indian who allegedly cured typhoid with the root.

Gravelroot has a tonic effect on the kidneys and a diuretic and anti-rheumatic action. It is a traditional remedy for rheumatism, gout, and gravel in the urinary system. Herbalists may also recommend it for cystitis and prostate trouble.

Hawthorn

Crataegus oxyacantha or *Crataegus monogyna*

May blossom, bread and cheese

Habitat Small native European tree. Introduced into other temperate zones, including North America. Found on heathland, chalk downs, and in open deciduous woods. Widespread in hedges, along roadsides, and field boundaries. Grown as an ornamental in parks and gardens.

Description Shrub or small tree from 4.5–9m (15–29ft) with greyish bark and tough, thorny branches, often gnarled. The small, dark green leaves are shiny and have three lobes. From May to June, clusters of small, creamy-white flowers with red anthers, and often tinged with pink, appear. They are followed by deep scarlet berries. **Parts used**: berries, leaves, flowers.

History The hawthorn usually blooms in May, and the Pilgrim Fathers' ship, the *Mayflower*, took its name from this tree. Haw is an old word for hedge or enclosure, and the hawthorn was considered the ideal tree for hedge planting, following the 19th-century English land enclosures. According to Christian legend, the crown of thorns was made from hawthorn twigs, and the famous Glastonbury thorn in southern England sprouted from the staff of Joseph of Aramathea. Many superstitions also grew up around this small tree: witches were said to shelter in hawthorn hedges, and to cut the wood down would bring either fairies or bad luck into the house.

Hawthorn is particularly valued for its strengthening and normalizing effect on the heart. In medical studies and research work, the berries lowered blood pressure by helping to dilate clogged and hardened arteries.

Hemlock

UMBELLIFERAE

Conium maculatum

Poison parsley

Habitat Native to southern and central Europe and widespread in temperate zones. Common in damp hedgerows, stream banks, moist, rough pastureland, and on waste ground.

Description Tall biennial similar to cow parsley and wild chervil, and growing to 2m (6ft) from a forked, pale yellow root. The stout, bright green stem is smooth and blotched with purple or deep red, and the delicate, dark green leaves are feathery and grouped in threes. The leaves have an unpleasant, 'mousy' smell when bruised. From mid-summer to mid-autumn, umbels of small, white, lacy flowers appear, followed by seeds (fruits) that resemble caraway.

History Hemlock's botanical name, *Conium*, is derived from a Greek verb that means to whirl around. This refers to the vertigo that is one of the characteristic symptoms of hemlock poisoning. Socrates and other condemned Greek criminals were forced to drink a deadly hemlock brew and it was a favourite drink of suicides. Witches also collected the plant for their potions.

Dioscorides prescribed the herb for the external treatment of herpes, and a poultice was once applied to cancerous tumours. The poisons were said to dissipate on cutting and drying. In the early part of this century, hemlock was an official sedative and antispasmodic drug, that was prescribed for epilepsy and other convulsive diseases. Today, hemlock is no longer employed medicinally due to the considerable variation in the strength of the herb, and the unpredictability of its effects.

CAUTION All parts are intensely poisonous.

Henbane

SOLANACEAE

Hyoscyamus niger

Stinking nightshade, hog's bean

Habitat Native to Europe. Introduced to Canada and northern USA, western Asia, and parts of South America. Grows wild on waste ground, in sandy places near the sea, and around derelict buildings and rubbish heaps.

Description Annual or biennial from 30–75cm (12–30in) with a powerful, nauseating smell. At the base of the stem the dull grey-green leaves are flat, oblong and coarsely indented; higher up the leaves are prominently veined, stalkless and a paler green. Both stems and leaves are sticky to the touch. From early to late summer, dull, buff-coloured, funnel-shaped flowers appear that are hairy and marked with lurid purple veins. The lids of the bean-like seed capsules that follow split open to reveal numerous small seeds. **Part used**: leaves.

History Henbane leaves have valuable sedative, pain-killing, and muscle-relaxing properties. In the first century AD, Dioscorides used henbane as a sleeping potion and pain killer, while during the Middle Ages smoking henbane seeds was a home remedy for toothache and rheumatic pain. The results of this home cure proved unpredictable and instances of delirium, convulsions and insanity were recorded. Henbane, like hemlock, was formerly an official sedative and analgesic. It is no longer used internally because of the risk of poisoning.

Henbane was widely employed in magical and satanic rites for its power to provoke hallucinations and convulsions. In 1910, the famous British murderer Dr Crippen poisoned his wife with henbane.

CAUTION All parts of the plant, especially the leaves, are poisonous.

Henna

Lawsonia inermis

Egyptian privet

Habitat Native to Arabic countries, Iran, India, and Egypt. Introduced and naturalized in North Africa and tropical parts of America. Cultivated for cosmetic use principally in Iran, Egypt and Morocco. Also grown as a garden ornamental.

Description Small shrub to 3m (10ft) with oblong or elliptical brownish-green leaves that resemble those of the privet. In summer, heavily perfumed white or red flowers bloom in broad, flattish clusters, followed by round berries.

Parts used: leaf, twigs.

History Examination of mummified remains from the tombs of ancient Egyptians has revealed that a mixture of henna and indigo, called 'reng', was used to colour hair and false beards. For centuries, Arabic women have dyed their hair, hands, feet and nails with the rich red pigment from the leaves. In the East, henna's redness symbolized the life-blood of the earth, and body-painting with henna was a means of connection with natural processes and cycles. It is still customary among certain orthodox Muslim and Hindu women to gather together to paint the bride's hands and feet with henna patterns on the eve of her wedding.

Today, a growing reaction against the harshness of some chemical hair colourings has led to the increased availability of plant-based hair colours. Powdered henna leaf produces a lovely shine and a rich red tone that fades naturally and will not harm the hair or scalp. The colour can be varied and darkened by mixing it with such dye plants as indigo, lucerne, and catechu. The best quality henna is said to come from Iran.

Hops

Humulus lupulus

Hop bine

Habitat Native to northern temperate zones, especially northern Europe, mountainous areas of southern Europe, and Britain. Widespread commercial cultivation in northern Europe. Introduced and cultivated in North America. Grows wild in damp hedgerows and thickets.

Description Well-known twinning, perennial vine with rough stems that climb to 6m (20ft). The long-stalked leaves with coarsely serrated margins are opposite and deeply indented. They are usually divided into three oval lobes that taper to a point. Yellowish-green flowers appear from late summer to mid-autumn: the female flowers are enclosed in cone-shaped catkins, and the male hang in loose bunches. The ripened female cones (fruits) are used for brewing beer.

Part used: flowers.

History Hops became an important flavouring for beer in 9th-century Europe, but the English resisted the introduction of the plant for a further eight centuries, calling it 'a wicked weed that would spoil the taste of the drink and endanger the people'. Brewers added hops to their beer primarily to extend its keeping qualities.

Hops contain a volatile oil and a bitter principle that have a soothing effect on the central nervous system, and are beneficialfor tension and anxiety. Many people report improved sleeping habits after using a pillow stuffed with dried hops. Hops also relax the bowel and ease nervous indigestion. Taken in large quantities, hops can interfere temporarily with male sexual function.

CAUTION Hops should be avoided by those suffering from depression.

Horse Chestnut

HIPPOCASTANACEAE

Aesculus hippocastanum

Habitat Native to mountainous areas of Greece and Albania. Introduced and widely cultivated in Europe, Britain and North America.

Description Deciduous tree to 35m (120ft) with stout trunk, greyish bark and spreading branches. The finely-toothed, bright green leaves are grouped in fives, like fingers. In early to late spring the sticky buds burst into erect cones or 'candles' of beautiful pinkish-white flowers. These are followed by globular, spiny, light green capsules containing a highly-polished brown fruit, popularly known as a 'conker'. **Parts used**: fruit, bark.

History The horse chestnut is not even distantly related to the sweet or Spanish chestnut, *Castanea sativa*. The origin of the prefix horse is uncertain but serves to distinguish the tree's bitter, inedible fruits from the edible, sweet variety. In rural areas of Eastern Europe, chestnuts are collected for horse and cattle fodder. Soaking removes the bitterness and the chestnuts are then ground into a fine meal.

Herbalists once employed an infusion of horse chestnut branch bark for fevers, and used the astringent fruits to treat rheumatism. Today, herbalists attach particular importance to horse chestnut's strengthening and tonic action on the circulatory system, especially the veins. Horse chestnut ointment, which tones the vein walls and reduces inflammation, is considered an excellent remedy for haemorrhoids and varicose veins in the legs.

Horseradish

Cochlearia amoracia or *Amoracia rusticana*

Red cole

Habitat Probably native to south-eastern Europe. Widely cultivated in northern Europe and North America. May be found wild on banks and roadsides.

Description Perennial to 1m (3ft) with a thick, white tapering taproot. The large, stalked leaves resemble those of the dock but are shiny, lighter green and less tough. The margins are dentate and wavy. Small white flowers appear from mid-summer to mid-autumn. **Part used**: fresh root.

History Estimates of how long horseradish has been in cultivation vary from 2–3000 years. What is certain is that the plant was first used medicinally. The Danes served horseradish at the table but the English, who considered horseradish overpowering and more suited to labourers' stomachs, continued eating mustard with their meat until the mid-17th century. Fresh horseradish is pungent and grating the root has a similar effect to chopping onions: the volatile oils make your eyes water. It is believed to stimulate the appetite and aid the digestion.

Taken internally, horseradish's strong diuretic action is beneficial for kidney problems. Externally, a poultice of the fresh root stimulates the circulation and is a traditional home remedy for easing the pain of rheumatic joints and chilblains.

Growing tips Propagate by root division and plant out in spring in well-drained, well-manured soil in a sunny position. Once established, horseradish grows vigorously.

Horsetail

Equisetum arvense

Bottle brush, shave grass

Habitat Native to Europe and introduced to North America and other temperate regions around the world, with the exception of Australia and New Zealand. Widespread in moist meadows, on waste ground, and in sandy soils near water.

Description Perennial with two types of hollow stem. A fertile, pinkish stem appears first, growing to 20cm (8in) and producing a conical spike that sheds its spores and dies down. Yellowish-green sterile shoots then appear that reach 80cm (32in) and have thread-like, feathery branches growing from the stem joints. **Parts used**: stems.

History The horsetail, like the fern, has probably evolved very little since prehistoric times, except in terms of size. It resembles a miniature tree and, two hundred millennia ago, was considerably taller. It may have been one of the dominant plant species of prehistoric earth.

Horsetail is rich in silica and in Medieval times the stems were used to polish metal, hence the plant's old name pewterwort, as well as to sand and polish wood. Centuries later, dairy maids were using the dried stems to scour their milk pails. Medicinally, horsetail's high silica content helps to heal damaged lung tissue and was once recommended for lung problems. Herbalists value its strengthening effect on lifeless hair and brittle nails, while its diuretic and astringent properties are beneficial for such urinary problems as gravel, enlarged prostate, and cystitis.

Hyssop

Hyssopus officinalis

Habitat Native to central and southern Europe, and the USSR. Introduced and naturalized in North America. Grows wild on dry soils that are rocky or chalky.

Description Hardy, camphor-scented bushy herb or small shrub with branched, square stems to 60cm (2ft). The small, linear leaves are stalkless and grow in whorls at intervals along the stem. From early summer to early autumn, pretty royal blue, white, or pink flowers bloom in the leaf axils, forming dense spikes towards the top of the stem.

Part used: flowering plant.

History Hyssop's scent has been described as medicinal, and the earliest recorded use of the plant was as a strewing herb to cleanse the air in sickrooms. In the home, too, hyssop helped to disguise unpleasant smells. Its strong, sharp taste was a popular flavouring for meats and stews during the Middle Ages. Hyssop oil is one of the ingredients in the French liqueurs, Benedictine and Chartreuse.

Hyssop is rarely use in today's kitchen on account of its pronounced minty and rather bitter flavour, but its reputation as a valuable medicinal herb has been sustained. A syrup of the flowers and leaves, which contain an expectorant and antiseptic volatile oil, is a traditional home remedy for chest complaints, and herbalists still recommend a hyssop infusion for coughs, bronchitis and catarrh. Externally, a hyssop poultice is recommended for black eyes and bruising.

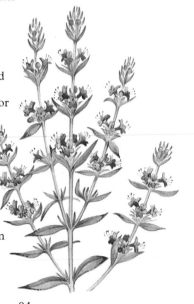

Growing tips Sow seed in rocky, well-drained to dry soil in spring in a sunny position. Hyssop is easy to grow and will attract bees.

Iceland Moss

Cetraria islandica

Iceland lichen

Habitat Widespread in cool,
mountainous northern regions
including North America,
Britain, northern and central
Europe. Grows in cool, damp
forests on stony ground.
Description Leafy lichen
with branched, curly frond
(thallus) from 3–12cm (1–
5in). The colour varies from
greenish-brown to grey, and
the underside is paler and
flecked with white. **Part
used**: dried plant.

History Iceland moss, a lichen with
soothing and antiobiotic properties, was
once used to treat tuberculosis.

Irish Moss

Chondrus crispus

Carrageenan

Habitat Widespread on the
coastlines of north-western
Europe, especially the Atlantic
coast of Ireland. Collected
at low tide, principally in
Ireland and northern France.
Description Seaweed 10–30cm
(4–12in) that varies in colour when
fresh from greenish-yellow to brown.
The fronds are flattened and curled, and
turn a translucent yellow or whitish shade
when dry. Small oval sacs (fruiting bodies)
appear on the stems. **Part used**: dried plant.
History Irish moss produces a mucilage-rich gel that eases
coughs and bronchitis.

Iris, Florentine

IRIDACEAE

Iris fiorentina or *Iris germanica*

Orris, white flower de luce

Habitat Native of southern Europe, especially Italy, and naturalized in central Europe, Iran, and northern India. Grows wild on hilly slopes in sunny situations. Cultivated commercially, particularly in Italy.

Description Perennial on a thick rhizome with an erect flowering stem to 60cm (2ft), and characteristic sword-shaped leaves. The large flowers usually appear in pairs at the end of the stem from early to mid-summer, and have no scent. The petals are either white with a pale lilac tinge and a yellow 'beard', or pure white. **Part used**: dried rootstock.

History The white Florentine iris was first cultivated in medieval Florence for the pronounced violet scent of the dried rootstock, commonly known as orris. The sweet, powdered root was initially used to scent linen but was later employed in the cosmetic hair powders necessary to maintain ornate 18th-century hairstyles. Orris root contains a volatile oil that acts as a valuable fixative in perfumery and stabilizes the fragrance of pot pourris. Powdered orris root makes an excellent dry shampoo and may be used as a talcum powder.

Orris root juice is a violent purgative and is now seldom used medicinally.

Growing tips Propagate by root division and plant in deep, rich soil that does not retain moisture.

Jimson Weed

SOLANACEAE

Datura stramonium

Thornapple, mad apple, devil's apple

Habitat Probably native to Asia. Naturalized and widespread in North and South America, and throughout Europe. Uncommon in Britain. A familiar weed on waste ground, roadsides, in ditches, and field edges. Prefers sunny situations.
Description Foul-smelling plant with an erect, rubbery yellow-green stem from 1–1.5m (3–5ft) and spreading branches. The leaves are large, dark green and jagged. The upper surface is smooth, veined, and dark green; the underside is paler green. Throughout the summer, large white to pale blue trumpet-shaped flowers appear followed by green, spiny seed capsules that are oval in shape and burst open to reveal numerous dark brown seeds. **Part used**: dried leaves.
History Jimson weed is a powerful narcotic that produces hallucinations and double vision. Under the guidance of the shaman, Native Americans employed the herb in puberty rites and other sacred rituals. The name of the herb is thought to be a corruption of Jamestown in Virginia. Early American settlers considered jimson weed a dangerous plant and it became known as mad apple or the devil's apple. People feared that it would summon witches.

Jimson weed leaves and seeds contain valuable alkaloids that have a marked sedative effect on the central nervous system and a strong action on the respiratory organs. A tobacco made from the leaves was smoked to relieve asthma attacks, and the herb was widely used to control the muscular spasms characteristic of Parkinson's disease.
CAUTION All parts of the plant, especially the seeds, are poisonous.

Juniper

CUPRESSACEAE

Juniperus communis

Habitat Native to Europe. Extensively distributed worldwide from the USSR through Europe and across to North America, growing wild from the Arctic Circle southwards. Found abundantly on mountain slopes, in open coniferous woodland, on heathland and moorland.

Description Variable prickly evergreen occurring as a low, spreading shrub to 1m (3ft) or a small tree to 6m (20ft). The leaves are flattened to very sharp needles that occur in whorls of three. The upper surface of the leaves is grey-green to grey-blue. From late spring male and female flowers appear on separate trees. The male flowers are yellow and do not ripen. The female flowers are tiny, greenish cones that can take from two to three years to ripen into blue-black fleshy berries.

Parts used: berries.

History The name juniper is derived from the Dutch word for gin, *jenever*, and the spirit owes its characteristic flavour to juniper's volatile oil. Gin distillers once added hand-picked berries to the spirit.

Juniper is an important medicinal plant which, like many other strongly scented herbs, was thought to keep out evil spirits as well as disease. A juniper bush by the door would prevent witches gaining entrance. The berries contain an antiseptic and a strongly diuretic volatile oil that flushes out the kidneys. Herbalists prescribe juniper for cystitis, urethritis and gout. Externally, diluted oil of juniper eases aching muscles and rheumatic and arthritic pain, while steam inhalations relieve catarrh and congestion.

CAUTION Avoid juniper if you are pregnant or if you suffer from kidney problems.

Lady's Bedstraw

RUBIACEAE

Galium verum

Our Lady's bedstraw, cheese rennet

Habitat Native to Europe. Naturalized in southern Canada, the north and eastern USA, and coastal regions of Britain. Grows in dry, sandy pastures, banks and roadsides.
Description Perennial with slender, erect or creeping stems from 20–80cm (8–32in) that bear whorls of six to eight narrow, thread-like leaves. From early to late summer honey-scented bright yellow flowers appear in terminal spikes. **Parts used**: leaves and flowering stems.
History According to Christian legend, Mary made up Christ's bedding with the dried stems of this plant, and its white flowers turned to gold. Our Lady's bedstraw, usually shortened to lady's bedstraw, was also a popular strewing herb and mattress stuffing during the Middle Ages. The dried, flowering stems give off a sweet, hay-like scent on account of the coumarin – a compound also found in woodruff – in the plant. Cheese rennet, the herb's other country name, refers to the ancient practice, widespread throughout Europe until the early 19th century, of using the acidic juice of the stems to curdle milk for cheese making.

   Lady's bedstraw is no longer used in mattresses, but stuffing a pillow with the dried stems is said to promote sound sleep. The active principles of the herb are similar to those of its relative, cleavers *Galium aparine*. Lady's bedstraw checks the flow of blood, and Culpeper recommended it for internal and external bleeding. For its mild sedative action, it was once one of the principal cures for hysteria.

Lady's Mantle ROSACEAE

Alchemilla vulgaris

Lion's foot

Habitat Native to northern Europe and at high altitudes in central and southern Europe. Lady's mantle is found in open woods and grassland.

Description Graceful, entirely green plant to 30cm (12in) covered with fine hairs. The large, lower leaves have long stalks and are kidney- to paw-shaped with seven to nine lobes. The edges are sharply toothed. The upper leaves are less stalked and much smaller. Loose clusters of pretty, yellow-green flowers bloom from early spring to early autumn. **Parts used**: leaves and flowering stems.

History Lady's mantle takes its name from the fancied resemblance of its leaves to the scalloped edges of a lady's mantle or cloak. The plant was also associated with the Virgin Mary. *Alchemilla*, the botanical name of the plant, points to its old reputation as a magical herb. In the Middle Ages, alchemists attached great importance to the overnight dewdrops that collected in the funnel-shaped centre of the leaves, and used the precious liquid in their experiments.

Lady's mantle is a traditional wound-healing and astringent herb. Culpeper praised it lavishly and prescribed it for 'all wounds inward and outward'. The herb has continued its long association with ladies: modern herbalists recommend an infusion for excessive menstrual flow. Lady's mantle is also useful for diarrhoea.

Lavender LABIATAE

Lavandula officinalis or *Lavandula angustifolia*

English lavender

Habitat Native to the Mediterranean region and widely distributed in southern Europe. Naturalized in the southern USA. Found on stony, well-drained soils in sunny situations. Widely cultivated commercially, especially in the South of France and in Britain.

Description Bushy, very fragrant perennial with short woody stems to 80cm (32in). The leaves are grey-green to silver-grey. They are narrow, linear and covered with a layer of soft white hairs. From mid-summer to early autumn whorls of six to ten sweet-smelling mauve or pale lilac flowers appear in spikes towards the end of the long stalks. **Parts used**: flowers, oil.

History Lavender was well known to the ancient Greeks and Romans, and takes its name from the Latin *lavare*, to wash, after the practice of scenting bath and washing water with lavender. Lavender was first cultivated in England during the 16th century and this fragrant, well-loved garden flower was taken across the Atlantic by the Pilgrim Fathers.

Lavender has sedative properties and is a traditional remedy for faintness and hysteria. Herbalists still recommend the flowers or the oil for tension and nervous headaches. Lavender oil is particularly effective for healing burns and scalds, and makes an excellent antiseptic for cuts and sores. It was used to disinfect wounds up until World War I. Lavender is an insect repellant and sachets are still popular for scenting drawers and linen cupboards.

Growing tips Propagate from cuttings and start in cold frames. Transplant to light, stony soil in a sunny, sheltered position and protect from frost.

Lemon

Citrus limon

Habitat Probably native to northern India or South-east Asia. Introduced and widely cultivated in Mediterranean countries, California and Florida.

Description Small, very attractive tree from 3–6m (10–20ft) with greyish bark and stout spines where the leaf stalks join the branches. The pale green, evergreen leaves are oval with serrated edges. In the leaf axils grow clusters of five-petalled flowers that are white inside and pink- or purple-tinged outside. They are followed by the well-known sour, yellow fruit. **Part used**: fresh fruit.

History Lemon is derived from a Hindustani word that was translated into Arabic as *limun*. The lemon came to Europe by way of Persia and cultivation began in Greece courtesy of Arabian expertise.

In the days of long sea journeys, British ships were required by law to carry lemons or limes as prevention against scurvy. The fruit is an excellent source of vitamin C and has cooling properties. Lemon juice is a traditional remedy for sunburn, and it was once taken cold to relieve feverish conditions, including malaria. Today, hot lemon juice and honey is still a favourite home remedy for colds and its astringency is useful for sore throats. In the home, lemon juice may be used to descale kettles and acts as a mild bleach. Lemon extract is extensively used in cosmetic products.

Lettuce

Lactuca virosa

Wild lettuce, prickly lettuce

Habitat Native European plant that grows on banks and waste ground in dry soils.

Description Biennial with a strong odour that grows to 1.5m (5ft) with a rosette of oblong, rounded leaves and a stout stem that is pale green, branched, and often prickly towards the base. The dark green stem leaves are smaller. From mid-summer to mid-autumn, numerous pale yellow flowers appear. The cut plant exudes a milky juice. **Parts used**: leaves, juice.

History This wild ancestor of the cultivated garden lettuce was once extensively grown in Europe for its bitter, milky juice, popularly known as 'lettuce opium'. This juice is less potent than that of the opium poppy but possesses similar narcotic properties and a sedative effect. It was generally available in dried form and called lactuarium. It was substituted for opium in cough preparations, and supplies allegedly found their way to America where they served as an opium adulterant. In the late 18th century, lettuce extract was listed as an official drug in certain European countries, and employed to treat irritable coughs, whooping cough, and insomnia. Today, herbalists still use the dried leaves for nervous coughs and as a mild sedative.

The garden lettuce has taken many years to develop and breeders have succeeded in eradicating the bitterness from the plant. Lettuce opium has all but disappeared along with the bitter juice.

Lily of the Valley

LILIACEAE

Convallaria majalis

May lily

Habitat Native to Europe and East Asia and introduced in North America. Rare in the wild in Britain and may be found as an escape in North America in dry woodland, especially ash woods. Widely cultivated as a garden plant.

Description Very fragrant perennial from 10–20cm (4–8in) that bears a pair of wide, oval, prominently ribbed leaves. They are mid- to dark green and taper to a point. From late spring to early summer pretty pearl-white flowers hang down from the stem; they resemble small bells with scalloped edges, and smell very sweet. They are followed by red berries containing seeds. **Parts used**: leaves and flowers.

History Lily of the valley, despite its name, does not grow exclusively in valleys. According to English legend, the plant first bloomed in a wooded area of the south-east where St Leonard fought and killed a dragon.

Lily of the valley was used medicinally as early as the 4th century. In Russian folk medicine, the plant was a traditional remedy for dropsy caused by a weak heart. Modern herbalists consider lily of the valley a valuable, and safer, heart tonic than foxglove. The herb normalizes the heart and its diuretic action helps the body to flush out toxins and excess fluid.

Growing tips Sow seed in moist, chalky soil under trees or in semi-shade. Propagate by root division in autumn. The plant spreads rapidly.

CAUTION The berries are poisonous and the plant must only be used as directed by a qualified practitioner.

Lime

Tilia europea

Common lime, linden

Habitat Native to Europe, especially France. Grows in deciduous or mixed woodland on sandy soils and has been widely planted in parks and gardens, as well as along city streets and avenues.

Description Large, domed deciduous tree to 25m (81ft) that is very fragrant when in blossom. The finely-toothed leaves are heart-shaped and taper to a sharp point. The upper surface is dark green and the undersides are paler. From mid- to late summer sweet-scented yellowish flowers with wing-shaped bracts hang in clusters from the branches. They are followed by small globular fruits. **Parts used**: flowers.

History Dried, honey-scented lime flowers make a pleasant tisane, the popular *tilleul* of France and *tiglio* of Italy. In the USA, Basswood tea, made from the American lime, has a similar, delicate flavour.

Lime tea is traditionally drunk as a digestive or, like chamomile, as an after-dinner drink to induce a peaceful night's sleep. The flowers have long been used in folk medicine to soothe anxiety and were considered helpful for hysteria, either taken as a tea or added to the bath water. During World War II, lime tea was prescribed for its mildly tranquillizing effect, and in parts of France lime tea is traditionally given to excitable and overactive children. Herbalists continue to recommend lime blossom for nervous tension and insomnia, and, since the flowers also promote perspiration, they are prescribed for feverish colds and flu, often in combination with elder flowers. Cosmetically, a lime blossom infusion improves the circulation and tones the skin.

Liquorice

Glycyrrhiza glabra

Spanish liquorice

Habitat Native to southern Europe, and from the Middle East to the USSR. Grows wild in the rich soil of river valleys, or on sandy soils. Widely cultivated in its native countries and also in California and Arizona.

Description Shrubby perennial from 50–150cm (20–60in) on a vertical, woody taproot that is yellow internally and sends out horizontal stolons. The graceful, pinnate leaves are in groups of 9 or 15, oval in shape and slightly sticky beneath. Spikes of pale blue, sweet-pea-like flowers appear from mid- to late summer, followed by small brownish-red seed pods.

Part used: root.

History Herbalists have been using liquorice for chest and throat complaints since the third century BC. The sweet-tasting root soothes inflammation, while its expectorant action helps to expel mucus. In addition, this valuable root has an antacid effect on the stomach, useful for alleviating heartburn, while its gel-like component assists in the healing of gastric ulcers. Liquorice, too, exhibits a similar action to the female hormone oestrogen, and has been used to alleviate menstrual cramps and menopausal conditions.

Commercially, the intense sweetness of liquorice has made it a common flavouring agent, especially for tobacco. Chewing the fibrous roots cleans and tones the teeth and gums.

Spain has long been a centre of liquorice cultivation. In England, the Dominican Black Friars began growing liquorice near Pontefract in Yorkshire.

CAUTION
Liquorice can cause salt and water retention. Avoid it if you suffer from high blood pressure or kidney problems.

Lobelia

Lobelia inflata

Indian tobacco, pukeweed

Habitat Native to Canada and the eastern USA. Found in dry pastures, on roadsides, and in open woodland.

Description Annual with branched, hairy stems from 30–60cm (1–2ft) that contain a milky, acrid juice. The light green leaves are stalkless, oval and have serrated edges. Numerous loose spikes of tubular, blue, lipped flowers appear from mid-summer. **Parts used**: stems and leaves.

History Native Americans smoked dried lobelia to relieve asthma and used it to treat dysentery. American settlers observed its medicinal properties and it was widely employed in New England, particularly by the Shakers, who exported it overseas. A noted 19th-century herbalist of the American physiomedical school, Samuel Thompson, promoted its use to relieve painful muscle spasms in childbirth, for epilepsy, diphtheria, and whooping cough. At that time the vomiting attacks that the herb provoked were considered cleansing, and this effect is reflected in the herb's common name, pukeweed.

Lobelia has a similar action on the nervous system to nicotine and the extract has been used in preparations to relieve withdrawal symptoms that follow giving up smoking tobacco. Some herbalists still recommend the herb for bronchitis, but others consider it unsafe since incorrect dosages can result in dangerously lowered blood pressure. It is, however, safe for external use, as a soothing rub for bruising, poison-ivy rash, and insect bites.

Lovage

Levisticum officinale

Love parsley

Habitat Native to southern Europe and naturalized in North America, particularly the eastern USA. Found in well-established herb gardens.

Description Perennial with fleshy root and stout, grooved, hollow stems to 1.5m (5ft). The leaves are glossy, dark green and similar in appearance and smell to wild celery. From early to mid-summer umbels of tiny yellow flowers appear followed by brownish, grooved, aromatic fruit. **Parts used**: root, stems, seed.

History Lovage, or love parsley, was a popular ingredient of love potions during the Middle Ages. The herb, particularly the root, has diuretic properties and was once important medicinally for the treatment of jaundice, kidney stones, and rheumatism. Culpeper considered lovage a stomach herb and recommended it to 'warm cold stomachs'. A tea of the root and seeds is a good digestive, and is still taken for stomach aches and kidney problems.

Lovage was popular with Benedictine monks during the Middle Ages, for its culinary as well as its medicinal properties. The leafy stems have a powerful, and somewhat unusual, celery-like flavour and may be used in soups and potato salads. Try sprinkling the salty seeds on bread and cheese biscuits. Lovage cordial, which contained more yarrow than lovage, was an old-fashioned English brew.

Growing tips Sow ripe seed in late summer to early autumn in well-drained, fertile soil in a sunny position. Keep moist in hot weather, prune well in autumn, and harvest after two years.

Lungwort

Pulmonaria officinalis

Jerusalem cowslip, spotted dog

Habitat Native to Europe and North America. Found on chalky soils in the shade of thickets and mixed woodland.

Description Perennial to 30cm (12in) that is bristly all over, like borage. The stalkless leaves have characteristic white spots and are oval to egg-shaped with a slight point. The tubular flowers share similarities with those of the cowslip or primrose. They turn from pink to blue, appearing from early to late spring. **Part used**: dried flowering plant.

History Adherents of the Doctrine of Signatures, prevalent in the 16th and 17th centuries, believed that the appearance of a plant indicated its medicinal application. Since the white-spotted leaves of the lungwort were thought to resemble diseased lungs, the plant was, accordingly, recommended for such pulmonary complaints as bronchitis. *Pulmonaria*, the Latin for lung and the botanical name of the genus, reflects its traditional medicinal use.

Analysis of the herb's constituents has, in fact, revealed that the mucilage and silica it contains are responsible for its soothing and expectorant properties. Four centuries later, herbalists continue to prescribe lungwort for bronchitis and other chest complaints. Lungwort is also rich in astringent tannins: lungwort tea is a folk remedy for diarrhoea and the leaves were applied to wounds.

Mandrake

Mandragora officinarum

Satan's apple

Habitat Native to south-east Europe, the Himalayas and Palestine. Grows on poor, sparse, sandy soils.

Description Perennial on stout, parsnip-like root that divides into two and resembles a pair of legs. The large, oval, foetid-smelling leaves to 30cm (12in), lie on the ground and have wavy margins. The five-petalled flowers appear on separate stalks and are whitish-yellow and tinged with purple. They are followed by round orange fruits that resemble a small apple.

Part used: dried root.

History Mandrake is a poisonous, hallucinogenic plant, long associated with magic. The fruits were found in Tutankhamun's tomb and the root was a favourite ingredient of witches' brews. The plant also had a reputation as a love potion and in the Old Testament it was employed as a fertility charm. According to legend, uprooting it was a perilous undertaking, since the plant uttered a piercing shriek that meant certain death. The task of pulling it up was, of necessity, entrusted to dogs. During the reign of Henry VIII, mandrake's human-shaped roots were thought to bring prosperity and changed hands for large sums.

Mandrake root has pain-killing properties. During the Middle Ages, it was infused in wine and administered as an anaesthetic during surgery. For its soporific effect, mandrake was used as a sedative and to ease rheumatic pains, convulsions, and nervous disorders. Today, mandrake is considered unsafe. The unrelated American mandrake or May Apple, *Podophyllum peltatum,* was once used as a laxative.

CAUTION Avoid. Both types are poisonous.

Marigold

Calendula officinalis

Mary bud

Habitat Native to southern Europe and parts of Asia. Introduced and distributed throughout northern temperate zones as a garden ornamental.

Description Familiar garden plant with a branching stem covered in fine hairs to 45cm (18in). The pale green, oblong leaves are hairy on both sides, with almost smooth edges. The lower leave are short-stalked, the upper leaves clasp the stem. In late spring, daisy-like flowers with a double row of orange-yellow petals appear. The curved fruits ripen from green to brown. **Part used**: flower heads.

History Marigold is a most useful herb with a long flowering period. This is reflected in its botanical name *Calendula*, from the Latin for the first day of every month. Looking upon marigolds was supposed to strengthen the eyesight, and the flowers were used to treat a range of ailments from headaches to red eyes and fevers.

Modern herbalists, and also homeopaths, consider marigold a valuable healing herb, and the ointment makes an excellent first-aid remedy for cuts, inflammations, bruises, and burns. A wash is soothing for sore, irritated eyes.

Marigolds were traditionally added to soups and stews, and used to colour cheese yellow. Dried and powdered, they make a good saffron substitute. The versatile marigold is also a cosmetic: a strong infusion of the petals heals and tones blemished skins, and makes a softening hair rinse for brunettes and redheads.

Growing tips Sow seed in a sunny position in spring, then thin out seedlings. Marigolds grow well in ordinary well-drained garden soil and need little attention.

Marjoram, Sweet

LABIATAE

Origanum marjorana

Knotted marjoram

Habitat Native to North Africa and South-west Asia. Introduced and naturalized in the Mediterranean and Central Europe. Cultivated in North America and north-western Europe.

Description Spicy and aromatic perennial, usually grown as an annual, with square, branching stems from 30–60cm (12–24in). Sometimes grows to the size of a small shrub. The rounded leaves are opposite, greyish and downy. From late summer to mid-autumn spherical, close heads of tiny white or pink flowers appear followed by tiny nutlets.

Part used: leaves.

History This popular herb's common name, knotted marjoram, describes the curious, knotted shape of the flower buds. Marjoram has been cultivated for centuries as a medicinal and a culinary herb, and was introduced into Europe during the Middle Ages. In ancient Greece, marjoram was a celebrated joy-bringer, that would comfort both the living and the dead. It was a customary to crown newly wed couples with marjoram, and if the herb grew on a tomb, it was a sign that the souls of the dead would find peace and happiness.

Marjoram's principal use is culinary, and its warm, spicy flavour both complements and aids the digestion of meat. In Germany, the herb is popularly known as *wurstkraut*, or sausage herb. Fresh marjoram has a subtle aroma that is easily lost after lengthy cooking, but the dried herb is more robust.

Growing tips Sow seed indoors or in a cold frame in early spring. Germination may be slow. Plant out in late spring in rich, well-drained soil, in a warm, sunny and very sheltered spot. Protect from frost and water sparingly.

Marjoram, Wild or Oregano

Origanum vulgare   LABIATAE

Habitat Native to Europe and found from Iran westwards to Central Asia. Found on dry, stony soils on hillsides, banks and roadsides to 2000m (6500ft). Collected commercially in Italy and naturalized in the north-eastern USA. Found on chalk downs or limestone in Britain.

Description Aromatic perennial, frequently bushy, with erect, hairy and woody stems to 60cm (2ft). The opposite greyish leaves are in pairs, with each pair at right angles to the next. They are broadly oval, pointed at the tip, and the upper leaves often have a reddish tint. From late summer to mid-autumn, two-lipped pinkish-purple or white flowers bloom in short, terminal spikes. **Part used**: flowering plant.

History For medicinal application, wild marjoram, or oregano, is considered more effective than sweet marjoram. The chemical constituents of the plant include antiseptic thymol, and the herb also has anti-inflammatory, expectorant and digestive properties. The Greeks applied wild marjoram poultices to sores, aching muscles and rheumatic joints. Wild marjoram tea was drunk by American settlers for respiratory ailments and as a digestive for upset stomachs. Today, herbalists recommend the herb for coughs, colds and flu, and as an antiseptic mouthwash for mouth and throat infections. The diluted oil eases muscular pains.

In the kitchen, wild marjoram is more usually referred to as oregano. It is used dried and gives pizza and spaghetti sauces their characteristic flavour.

Growing tips In cooler climates the true flavour of wild marjoram does not develop. For culinary use, plant sweet marjoram.

Marshmallow

Althaea officinalis

Sweet weed

Habitat Native to Europe and naturalized in the eastern USA. Commonly found in estuaries and salt marshes; also found in damp meadows and marshy wasteland.

Description Erect perennial from 1–1.25m (3–4ft) with a stout, tapering taproot that is yellowish on the outside. The stem and leaves are covered with soft hairs, and the greyish-green leaves are similar to those of the hollyhock – rounded to triangular, pointed and irregularly serrated. From mid-summer to early autumn five-petalled pale-pink or white flowers bloom in the leaf axils, followed by round, flattish fruits known as 'cheeses'. **Parts used**: root and leaves.

History *Althaea*, marshmallow's botanical name, is from the Greek word for cure. All parts of the plant, especially the root, are rich in mucilage that soothes and heals soreness and inflammation. Early Arab physicians used marshmallow poultices to heal inflammations, and the ancient Greeks employed it for wounds, ulcers and stings. Marshmallow syrup is a traditional remedy for coughs, bronchitis and sore throats. Today, herbalists prescribe the root for stomach ulcers and urinary tract inflammations. Externally, a warm marshmallow poultice is helpful for ulceration of the legs.

Marshmallow root is sweetish, but bears no resemblance to the sugary confectionery that is toasted over campfires. Its gelatin-like juice was, however, included in confectioners' pastes and lozenges.

Growing tips Sow the seeds in a sunny but damp spot. Protect from frost during the winter.

Meadowsweet

Filipendula ulmaria or *Spirea ulmaria*

Queen of the meadow, meadwort

Habitat Native to Europe and Asia and introduced and naturalized in North America. Grows on moist, rich soils on the banks of streams and rivers, as well as in marshes and damp meadows.

Description Familiar perennial from 60–120cm (2–4ft) with stiff, reddish stems. The alternate, aromatic, feather-like leaves are toothed with two to five pairs of leaflets. They are dark green above and greyish-white beneath. Dense plumes of sweet-smelling, cream-coloured flowers bloom from mid-summer to early autumn, followed by spiral-shaped fruit. **Part used**: flowers.

History Meadowsweet flowers have a sweet, warm, almond scent, while the leaves are sharper and more aromatic. In 14th-century England, the leaves were used to add extra flavour to the honey-based drink known as mead, and also added to wine and port.

Gerard prescribed meadowsweet for ague, and the fever-reducing properties of the plant were scientifically proven in 1839 when salicylic acid was found in the flower buds. This substance, synthesized in 1889, was named aspirin, – a derivative of meadowsweet's botanical name, *Spirea*. Salicylic acid has anti-inflammatory properties and can also lower the temperature. Herbalists recommend meadowsweet for rheumatic and arthritic pain, and for feverish colds and flu. In cases of heartburn and acid stomach, meadowsweet, unlike aspirin, does not irritate the stomach lining.

Growing tips Grow from seed sown in spring or autumn, or propagate by dividing the roots in spring. Meadowsweet prefers damp, rich soil with some shade, and will flourish near water.

Mint, Peppermint
Mentha piperita

Habitat Native to Europe and Asia. Widely distributed and naturalized in North America. Found in hedgerows, on the banks of streams, and on waste ground near dwellings. Rarely occurs in the wild in Britain.

Description A hybrid between spearmint (*Mentha spicata*) and water mint (*Mentha aquatica*). Familiar perennial with erect, square, and slightly hairy stem from 60–90cm (2–3ft). The oval, very aromatic, toothed leaves have pointed tips and are smooth and dark to reddish green. From late summer to mid-autumn elongated conical spikes of pinkish to mauve flowers grow at the tops of the stems.

Part used: flowering plant.

History In Greek myth Minte, a nymph, was pursued by Pluto, whose jealous wife turned her into a low-growing plant. The mint, although trodden underfoot, smelled sweet.

Herbalists attach particular importance to peppermint's menthol content. This valuable aromatic compound has cooling, antispasmodic, antibacterial, anaesthetic and decongestant properties. Peppermint tea is an excellent digestive and pick-me-up, and its antispasmodic action helps to alleviate menstrual cramps. Peppermint also stimulates the digestion, hence the tradition of after-dinner mints, while the antiseptic oil is widely employed in toothpaste. The menthol extracted from peppermint is commonly included in rubs for aching muscles and joints. For colds and catarrh, peppermint inhalations clear the head and chest.

Growing tips Propagate by dividing the roots in spring and put into water to root. Plant out cuttings in moist, rich soil in a sheltered and partially shaded position. Cut back regularly.

Spearmint

Mentha spicata

Garden mint

Habitat Native to southern Europe and western Asia. Widely distributed. May be found wild as an escape in moist, fairly shady positions near habitation. Cultivated extensively.

Description Perennial with straight, square stems to 60cm (2ft) and short-stalked, sharply pointed, bright green leaves that are narrower and more lance-shaped than those of peppermint. The leaf edges are finely toothed and the undersides prominently ribbed. From early autumn narrow, tapering spikes of pinkish flowers grow at the top of the stem.

Part used: flowering plant.

History This well-known culinary herb was introduced and promoted by the Romans who were very partial to its flavour. The naturalist Pliny declared that 'the smell of Mint doth stir up the minde and the taste to a greedy desire of meate'. Spearmint is a traditional English herb and has been grown in kitchen gardens since the 9th century. This herb was probably introduced into North America by the Pilgrim Fathers, and soon became established. In English cookery, mint sauce is the classic accompaniment to roast lamb, and chopped mint is served with new potatoes, peas, and young carrots. In the southern USA, mint julep – a concoction based on fresh spearmint leaves, bourbon, and crushed ice – became a fashionable, cooling cocktail during the 19th century.

Medicinally, spearmint has similar properties to peppermint but its effects are weaker. Spearmint was considered more appropriate for children's ailments and sweetened spearmint tea was used to treat upset stomachs, hiccups, and vomiting.

Growing tips As for peppermint.

Mistletoe

Viscum album

Birdlime, European mistletoe

Habitat Native to north-west Europe, extending south to the Mediterranean and eastwards as far as China. American mistletoe *Phoradendron serotinum* grows from New Jersey southwards as far as Texas. Found on deciduous trees, especially the apple. American mistletoe prefers juniper trees.

Description Well-known evergreen parasite that takes root on the branches of deciduous trees, especially those with soft bark. A bushy, spherical, shrub with woody, yellowish-green stems to 1m (3ft) that fork into many branches. The narrow, bluntly oval leaves are a dull yellow-green and leathery in texture. From mid-spring to early summer small, inconspicuous flowers appear in the leaf axils and are followed by the familiar sticky, pearl-like berries that ripen in December. **Parts used**: leafy twigs.

History In pre-Christian times, mistletoe, a plant that sprouted mysteriously from trees, was endowed with magical powers. For the oak-worshipping Druids, mistletoe berries symbolized the seed of the oak god, and the plant was important medicinally, and in fertility rites. At the winter solstice, the mistletoe was ritually cut down with a golden sickle to symbolize the death of the old year and the rebirth of the new. The custom of kissing under the mistletoe goes back to the Druidic fertility rites.

Mistletoe berries are poisonous to humans but not to birds. Seventeenth-century herbalists used the leafy branches to treat nervous convulsions, and modern analysis has confirmed the plant's sedative action. Mistletoe also helps to lower blood pressure and researchers are currently studying the plant's anti-tumour activity.

CAUTION The berries are poisonous.

Motherwort

LABIATAE

Leonorus cardiaca

Lion's tail

Habitat Native to Europe and introduced into the northern USA Found on banks, in hedgerows, along pathways, and on waste ground. Rare in Britain.

Description Pungent-smelling perennial on stout, erect stem from 1–1.5m (3–5ft), that may be purple-tinted. The downy leaves occur in opposite pairs up the stem and are divided into three to five deeply incised lobes. From mid-summer to mid-autumn whorls of bristly, pinkish-white flowers appear in the leaf axils. **Part used**: flowering plant.

History Motherwort is a traditional women's remedy for stress following childbirth.

Mountain Grape

BERBERIDACEAE

Mahonia aquifolium

Oregon grape

Habitat Native to British Columbia and extending southwards from Oregon to Idaho and Colorado. Grows under coniferous trees on mountain slopes. Naturalized in Europe, and a popular garden shrub.

Description Evergreen shrub from 1–3m (3–6ft) on brownish, knotty root with dense foliage. The leathery, dark green leaves are holly-like with prickly edges, and turn golden in autumn. The flowers are tiny, bright yellow and strongly scented. They are followed by dark bluish-purple berries. **Part used**: root.

History Herbalists recommend the bitter, dried root for a variety of skin problems.

Mugwort

COMPOSITAE

Artemisia vulgaris

St John's herb, Moxa

Habitat Native to Asia and Europe. Introduced and naturalized in North America as far south as Georgia and west to Michigan. Common on waste ground, on roadsides, and in hedgerows and ditches.

Description Erect perennial to 1m (3ft) with downy and grooved stems that are tinged with purple. The upper leaves have a faintly sage-like scent and resemble wormwood except that the leaf segments have pointed, not blunted tips. They are pinnate and deeply incised, dark green above and a downy grey beneath. From late summer to mid-autumn, long, terminal spikes of brownish-yellow to reddish flowers with five stamens appear; these are followed by stick-like seeds.

Part used: leafy stems.

History The English name of the plant is said to reflect its old use as a flavouring for home-brewed ale. In the Middle Ages, mugwort was associated with John the Baptist, and was worn on St John's Eve as a protection against evil spirits. In China, too, bunches of mugwort were hung in the home during the Dragon Festival in the belief that they would drive out demons.

For centuries mugwort has been valued for its regulating effect on the menstrual cycle, and a mugwort compress was used in childbirth to aid expulsion of the placenta. Externally, dried mugwort eases aching muscles, and relieves rheumatic pain. Acupuncturists burn cones made from the downy leaf fibres close to the skin to stimulate acupuncture points – a technique known as moxibustion.

Growing tips Sow seed indoors to help germination, then plant out seedlings in ordinary to poor garden soil in a sunny position.

Mullein, Great

SCROPHULARIACEAE

Verbascum thapsus

Torches, donkey's ears

Habitat Native to Europe and temperate Asia. Naturalized along the US Atlantic coast, and common throughout the eastern states as far west as South Dakota. Grows on roadsides, in hedgerows, on waste ground, and grassy banks.

Description Rigid, erect biennial that grows from a basal rosette of large, woolly leaves up to 2m (6ft) in the second year. The stout stems bear large, thick, foxglove-like leaves and both stem and leaves are covered on both sides with a soft grey felt. The leaves clasp the stem and have wavy margins. From mid-summer to early autumn, long, dense spikes of cup-shaped, lemon-yellow flowers appear with five rounded petals.

Parts used: leaves and flowers.

History Mullein's tall, dried stems were dipped in tallow to make tapers, hence the name torches. Another common name, Candlewick plant, refers to the rural custom of collecting and drying the down from the leaves and stems to make wicks for candles. The country name, hag's taper, means hedge candle. Hag also means witch and since witches sheltered in hedges, they probably knew how to make mullein candles.

Mullein leaves are rich in mucilage and were smoked to ease chest complaints. The flowering plant also has antispasmodic and expectorant properties, which explains its traditional role in treating asthma and consumption. Herbalists still recommend mullein for a wide range of respiratory ailments. Drops made by macerating the blossoms in warm olive oil are a folk remedy for earache.

Growing tips Sow seed in spring in well-drained, preferably stony soil in a sunny position.

Mustard, Black

CRUCIFERAE

Brassica nigra

Habitat Native to Europe, Asia Minor, China, India, North Africa, North and South America. Widespread throughout the world and found in hedges, on waste ground, roadsides, and sometimes on sea cliffs. Limited commercial cultivation.

Description Erect annual to 2m (6ft) with bluish-green to grass-green leaves and much branched stems. The leaves are alternate and the lower are stalked, lobed and coarsely toothed. The shape varies from spear-shaped to oval or elliptic. From summer to early autumn small, aromatic, bright yellow flowers are borne on twig-like stems. They have four rounded petals in the shape of a cross. These are followed by smooth, beaked seed pods that contain reddish-brown seeds.

Part used: seed.

History Black mustard, a coarser and more pungent variety than white or brown, was popular with the ancient Greeks and Romans: they simply ground it on to their food and made salads of the young leaves. Meat-eaters in Medieval England flavoured a runny sauce of mustard, honey and olive oil. In 1634 mustard from the French city of Dijon was officially licensed.

Black mustard has been used medicinally since classical times, principally for its warming and stimulating properties. In North America, the Mohegan Indians treated headaches and toothache with black mustard, while early settlers used mustard ointment to ease rheumatic pain. Applying mustard poultices to the chest eases stubborn coughs, and mustard plasters bring relief to aching joints. A hot mustard footbath is a time-honoured home remedy for colds and poor circulation.

Growing tips See White Mustard.

CAUTION Mustard may irritate sensitive skin.

Mustard, White

CRUCIFERAE

Brassica alba

Yellow mustard

Habitat Native to the Mediterranean region and western Asia. Introduced elsewhere. Originally an escape, now found wild in Britain and North America. Cultivated commercially.
Description Annual to 1m (3ft) with bright green slightly hairy stems and alternate, pinnate leaves. The largest leaves are usually divided into three lobes with coarsely and irregularly toothed margins. From mid-summer to early autumn appear small lemon-yellow flowers like those of black mustard and with a similar smell. These are followed by horizontal, bristly seed pods that are ribbed, swollen, and beaked at the tip. They contain yellow seeds. Black mustard seed pods are erect and smooth. **Part used**: seed.
History In the USA, white mustard forms the basis of the mild, yellow, hot-dog mustard. Some English mustards contain the white seed but Dijon mustard is based on the black and brown (*Brassica juncea*) varieties. White mustard is commonly used whole in pickling, both for its flavour and to extend the pickle's keeping qualities. Young mustard seedlings are popular in salads: they are the mustard part of mustard and cress, although today rape seedlings are often substituted.

White mustard has similar medicinal applications to black mustard and the two may be mixed. White mustard may also be taken as a tea or added to the bath for feverish colds and influenza.
Growing tips Sow seed in spring in a sunny position in rich, well-drained soil. White mustard is said to tolerate heavier soils than the black variety. Thin seedlings to 20cm (8in) and add compost regularly. Mustard self-seeds so harvest before the seed pods split open.

Nasturtium

Tropaeolum majus

Garden nasturtium, Indian cress

Habitat Native to South America, especially Peru. Widely cultivated as a garden ornamental.

Description Climbing perennial to 3m (9ft). Grown as an annual in cooler climates. The twining stems bear pale green, almost round leaves that are veined and have long stalks. From early summer to late autumn, trumpet-shaped flowers appear. They have spurs at the base and range from orange-yellow to deep orange-red. **Parts used**: flowers and leaves.

History The Spanish Conquistadors brought the Peruvian nasturtium to Europe in the 16th century, and it reached England at the end of that century. The nasturtium soon became a popular flower in European gardens, and in the kitchen. People enjoyed the watercress-flavoured young leaves and the peppery-tasting petals, and added them to salads. The young flower buds may also be pickled and eaten like capers. Nasturiums were a feature of many American colonial gardens and Thomas Jefferson, a keen herb grower, was very partial to them. When he was President, his garden at Monticello featured a vast nasturtium bed measuring 158 sq m (190 sq yds).

Nasturium leaves and flowers are mildly antibacterial and were once prescribed for genito-urinary infections and such respiratory ailments as bronchitis. The fresh leaves are rich in Vitamin C, especially if they are picked before the plant flowers, and they were traditionally eaten as a preventive against scurvy.

Growing tips Sow seed in early spring in a sunny location, in a l ight, well-drained soil. Nasturtiums also make good pot plants and will flourish on a sunny windowsill.

Nettle

Urtica dioica and *Urtica urens*

Stinging nettle

Habitat Native to temperate regions of Europe and Asia.
Distributed worldwide and naturalized in North America from
Newfoundland westwards to Colorado and southwards to
South Carolina. Grows on waste ground, in hedgerows,
ditches, against walls and fences, and in gardens.
Description Familiar perennial from 90–180cm (3–6ft) with
a single bristly stem, sparsely branched. The dull, dark green
leaves are similar to those of mint. They are opposite, heart-
shaped, and taper to a point. The surface is covered with
bristly, stinging hairs and the margins are finely toothed. From
mid-summer to mid-autumn, clusters of greenish, catkin-like
flowers appear. *U. urens*, the lesser nettle, grows to only 1m
(3ft). It is less downy than *U. dioica*, with smaller leaves and
flowers. **Part used**: leaves.
History The nettle takes its name from an old Anglo-Saxon
or Dutch word *noedl* meaning needle – either on account of its
sharp sting, or its fibre content. For centuries, nettles were
woven into cloth, coarse sheets, and even fishing nets.

The nettle's long history of medicinal
application included the curious
practice of urtication – thrashing
painful arthritic limbs with the fresh
stems, which act as a counter-
irritant. Roman soldiers
stationed in Britain and
numbed with cold,
reputedly applied nettles to
restore the circulation.
Nettles have a high iron
and vitamin C content,
useful in cases of anaemia,
and a cleansing spring
tonic was once made from
the young tops. Home-
brewed nettle beer eased
rheumatic pains, and
nettle tea is still
considered helpful for
arthritis and gout.
Nettles are also a
traditional cure for falling hair.

Nutmeg and Mace

Myristica fragrans

Habitat Native to Indonesia, particularly the Moluccas, Malaysia and the Philippines. Introduced and cultivated in other parts of the tropics including the West Indies. Grows in shady locations in areas with a high degree of humidity, and on volcanic soils.

Description Tall evergreen tree to 9m (30ft) that appears bushy and flowers after around nine years. The bark is greyish brown and smooth in texture. The spreading branches bear aromatic, glossy, dark green leaves that are elliptical in shape and taper to a point. Umbels of yellowish male and female flowers appear in the leaf axils of separate trees and are followed by hanging, yellow or red plum-like fruit. On ripening and drying, the fruit splits open to reveal a brilliant red membrane or aril – mace – which encases the nutmeg.

Parts used: seed and outer casing (mace).

History Nutmeg and mace were known to both the Indians and the Arabs during the 6th century. By the 12th century, this spice had reached Europe and it was among the aromatic and fumigant herbs and spices scattered in the streets of Rome for Henry VI's coronation. Supplies of nutmeg were limited until the early 16th century when the Portuguese opened up a direct sea route to the East.

Nutmeg, like many common kitchen spices, has digestive properties and can alleviate nausea and flatulence. In small doses nutmeg is mildly soporific, which explains its traditional inclusion in milky nightcaps. In moderate to large doses, however, nutmeg is hallucinogenic, due to an active ingredient, myristicin, with a similar effect to mescalin.

CAUTION Use nutmeg sparingly. Large doses can be fatal.

Oak

FAGACEAE

Quercus robur

English oak, tanners bark

Habitat Native to Britain and northern Europe. Introduced elsewhere. Grows on moist, heavy clay soils but will tolerate sandy soils. Found in mixed woodland and lowland regions. The white oak *Quercus alba* is a North American native that is also used medicinally.

Description Familiar, robust deciduous tree to 40m (130ft) with a rounded, spreading crown and smooth, greyish bark that develops fissures with age. The oblong leaves have three to seven lobes on each side and with them appear catkin-like flowers. In autumn the fertile female flowers produce the familiar greenish-brown acorns sitting in their cups. **Parts used**: bark, leaves, acorns.

History In Norse, Greek, Roman and Celtic mythologies the tree is the symbolic dwelling place of the principal male god, and signifies both strength and fertility. For the Vikings, the oak was Thor's sacred tree and offered protection from lightning. In Celtic Britain the oak was initially worshipped by the Druids. With the establishment of Christianity, gospels were commonly preached beneath its shade and an area of North London still bears the name Gospel Oak.

In medieval folklore, touching an afflicted part of the body with a nail, and then driving the nail into an oak was considered a cure for illness. The leaves were once applied to cuts. Today, herbalists use only the bark. Its powerful astringency is helpful for acute diarrhoea, while its antiseptic action is useful for treating throat infections. Edible acorns were commonly roasted and ground to make coffee.

Oats

Avena sativa

Groats

Habitat Origin uncertain. *Avena sativa* is cultivated commercially all over the world, particularly in the USSR, North America and Scotland. It is often found wild as an escape.

Description Annual tufted grass from 60–120cm (2–4ft) with a smooth, hollow, jointed stalk. The broad, flat, pale green leaves are rough in texture and taper to a point, and flowers are borne in small spikes at the end of the stems. After the flowers, swaying seed heads appear that contain the edible, grooved grain. **Parts used**: grain and straw.

History Oats are an ancient food plant and a source of important nutrients. Sixty years ago, 25 species of oats were cultivated. Today only three species remain. Oats have long been an important feature of the Scottish diet, and oatmeal cakes and porridge are traditional fare. Although the popularity of porridge has declined, many Europeans start the day with an oat-based cereal, such as muesli.

Oats, which are rich in the B group vitamins, tone and strengthen the nervous system, and herbalists recommend the grains for easing stress and tension. In convalescence or for gastro-intestinal problems, porridge or gruel makes a nourishing and easily digested food. Oatstraw tea is a traditional remedy for chest complaints. Externally, an oatmeal poultice will soothe allergic skin conditions, or try an oatmeal bath bag. Fill a muslin bag with oatmeal, soak it in the bath, then gently rub it over your skin. Oatmeal also makes an excellent facial scrub.

Olive

Olea europea

Habitat Native to the Mediterranean region, except Egypt. Olives have been introduced elsewhere and widely cultivated in warm to sub-tropical climates.

Description Small evergreen tree to 8m (25ft) with a slim trunk covered in greyish bark. The branches, often gnarled, bear opposite, lance-shaped leaves that are grey-green above and silvery beneath. Creamy, fragrant flowers appear in spring, followed by the familiar hard green oval fruit that ripens to dark purple. **Parts used**: fruit and oil.

History The olive has been cultivated for over 3000 years and its Latin name *Olea*, is the origin of the word oil. The tree was sacred to Athena, and sprang out of the ground when the city of Athens was founded. The olive is a symbol of plenty and its branch a sign of peace. According to the Old Testament, Moses decreed that those who tended the olive groves were excused from military service. Olive oil has been used in cooking for centuries. The best quality is pale yellow-green in colour and has a fine flavour. It is produced from the first cold pressing of fresh, ripe olives.

Olive oil has a laxative action and is reputed to lower blood cholesterol levels. Externally, warm olive oil dropped in the ear helps to relieve earache, and makes a soothing massage for aching muscles. For dry, damaged hair, try rubbing in olive oil and leave it on overnight. In folk medicine, a strong infusion of the astringent leaves served as an antiseptic for wounds, and was also taken for fevers.

Pansy, Wild

VIOLACEAE

Viola tricolor

Heartsease

Habitat Native to Europe and naturalized in North America. Grows in hedgerows, on cultivated grassland, and wood edges.
Description Annual or perennial to 15cm (6in) with a soft, hollow stem and spoon-shaped, opposite leaves with rounded lobes, not heart-shaped like those of the violet. The pansy-like flowers vary in colour and are usually a mixture of bright purple, white, and yellow. The lower petal is spurred at the base. **Part used**: flowering plant.
History Pansy, derived from the French word for thought, *pensée*, was a popular ingredient of love potions. As its common name, heartsease, suggests, the flower was reputed to alleviate the pain of separating from a loved one. In *A Midsummer Night's Dream*, it was the juice of this flower that inspired Titania with a passion for Bottom, the weaver.

In herbal medicine, wild pansy is a traditional remedy for such skin disorders as acne, eczema, and psoriasis. Externally, it is considered gentle enough for treating cradlecap in babies. The plant also has other valuable medicinal properties applicable to a variety of ailments. Wild pansy is both diuretic and anti-inflammatory and has been used to treat urinary problems, gout and arthritis. The herb, too, has a soothing and expectorant action, which accounts for its reputation as a remedy for respiratory ailments.

Parsley

Petroselinum crispum

Curly-leaved parsley

Habitat Native to the Mediterranean. Introduced and naturalized elsewhere, particularly in Britain, north and central Europe. May be found wild in rocky places as an escape. Widely cultivated.

Description Familiar biennial to 60cm (2ft) on a stout taproot with branching stems. The bright green leaves are deeply segmented and tightly curled over. In the second year, umbels of tiny greenish-yellow flowers appear in early summer; these are followed by small, ribbed fruits (seeds). The flat-leaved variety has more feathery, celery-like leaves that lie flat and are a darker shade of green.

Parts used: leaves, root, and seed.

History To the ancient Greeks, curly-leaved parsley was a plant of death, and the leaves were customarily scattered over corpses, or made into wreaths. In European folklore, parsley's lengthy germination period fostered the belief that, before the plant would grow, its roots had to go down to the devil seven times.

Herbalists consider parsley a kidney and liver tonic, as well as a digestive, and a tea is helpful for bladder problems, rheumatism and flatulence. Parsley is a highly nutritious herb: it is a rich source of vitamin C, plus iron, calcium, and vitamins A and B. This ubiquitous culinary and garnishing herb also acts as a breath freshener. Try chewing a sprig after eating onions or garlic.

Growing tips Sow seed in early summer in a rich, moist soil where there is a little shade. Encourage germination by pre-soaking the seed in warm water, and water well in hot weather.

Parsley Piert

Aphanes arvensis

Breakstone, field lady's mantle

Habitat Native to Britain and common in Europe in fields, on stony, waste ground, and on the top of stone walls.
Description Low-growing, delicate annual with short, slender stems to 15cm (6in). The small, bright green, wedge-shaped leaves are divided into between three and five lobes and deeply incised. The whole plant is downy and bears tufts of tiny, inconspicuous, greenish flowers from spring to late summer. **Parts used**: leaves and flowers.
History Parsley piert bears a vague resemblance to parsley, but the two species are not related. The herb takes its common name from the French, *perce-pierre*, meaning pierce-stone – a reference to the plant's habit of rooting in stone walls and stony ground. To the followers of the Doctrine of Signatures, parsley piert's ability to grow up through stones was a clear indication that it would dissolve urinary stones and gravel. Culpeper spoke highly of the plant and advised: 'You may take a drachm of the powder of it in sherry wine: it will bring away gravel from the kidneys insensibly and without pain'. Modern research has confirmed the herb's powerful diuretic action and herbalists still recommend parsley piert for the treatment of urinary infections, painful urination, kidney stones and urinary gravel.

In the Scottish Hebridean islands, parsley piert was traditionally pickled, like samphire, or eaten raw as a salad vegetable.

Pasque Flower

Anemone pulsatilla

Wind flower

Habitat Native to Europe and introduced elsewhere. Found wild on dry, grassy slopes and chalk downs throughout northern and central Europe. Grown as a garden ornamental.

Description Perennial from 10–25cm (4–10in) on a thick rootstock that sends up bunches or a rosette of finely divided leaves, and a slender flowering stem. Leaves, stems and flowers are covered with soft, silky hairs and most of the leaves develop after the flowers have appeared. The lovely six-petalled flowers appear on separate stems from late spring to mid-summer and are a matt, dark purple with yellow stamens. They are followed by attractive, fluffy seed heads.

Parts used: flowers and leaves.

History The common name, windflower, reflects the waving motion of the plant's frail stems when a breeze is blowing. Gerard christened the plant pasque flower because it blooms at Easter and prescribed it for watery, infected eyes. Indeed, the plant has long been associated with weeping. In Greek myth, the pasque flower sprouted from Aphrodite's tears, and homeopaths prescribe the plant for sensitive, weepy types and clingy, tearful children.

Pasque flower is a valuable remedy for female reproductive complaints. Its mild sedative action and muscle relaxant properties are helpful for menstrual cramps, especially when they are accompanied by tension or anxiety. Pasque flower may also be prescribed for ovarian pain and inflammation of the reproductive organs.

Growing tips Sow seed in spring in a light, well-drained, preferably chalky soil, choosing a sunny position.

CAUTION The fresh plant is poisonous and should only be taken as directed by a qualified practitioner.

Passionflower

Passiflora incarnata

Habitat Native to the southern USA from Florida westwards to Texas and north-westwards to Ohio. Found wild in thickets, along fences, and wood edges, where there is some shade. Widely cultivated.

Description Perennial hairy vine that climbs by means of coiling tendrils and grows from 3–9m (10–30ft). The woody stems bear alternate, lanceolate leaves that are divided into three finely toothed lobes. From early to late summer beautiful, sweet-scented flowers appear with five white to pale lavender petals and a striking, purple, ringed corona. These are succeeded by an edible, yellow to orange, oval fruit. **Parts used**: flowering plant and fruit.

History In the spectacular blossoms of the passionflower, the 17th-century Spanish colonists of South America saw the symbols of Christ's crucifixion. They interpreted its appearance as a divine blessing for their task of converting the indigenous peoples to Christianity.

Passionflower is a valuable sedative, and in the late 19th century, an extract of the plant was officially prescribed for insomnia, hysteria, seizures and nervous exhaustion. The plant was smoked for its mild narcotic effect and some considered the flower an aphrodisiac. Today, herbalists value passionflower for its non-addictive tranquillizing properties and recommend it for recurrent insomnia, anxiety and tension. The fruit of this species, known as granadilla, is edible and is a popular ingredient of fruit juices.

Growing tips May be grown from seed or from cuttings in deep, fertile, well-drained soil. Water well and provide some shade from strong sunlight. In cooler climates passionflower may need the warmth of a greenhouse.

Pennyroyal

Mentha pulegium

European pennyroyal, pudding grass

Habitat Native to Europe and western Asia. Found on rich, moist and sandy soils, often in ditches, and near streams and pools. American pennyroyal, *Hedeoma pulegiodes*, found in fields and open woods, is common in the eastern USA.
Description Aromatic mint-like perennial, growing low along the ground or erect to 30cm (12in). The square, branching stems bear oval, slightly hairy, greyish-green leaves with serrated or scalloped edges and a pungent, minty scent. In late summer, two-lipped, lilac-blue flowers bloom from the leaf axils, forming dense whorls up the stem. American pennyroyal is a more upright plant that grows in dry soils, reaching 40cm (16in), and has longer leaves than the European variety. **Parts used**: leaves, oil.
History Pennyroyal's specific botanical name is from the Latin *pulex*, meaning flea, and in Roman times, the herb was a popular flea repellant. According to reports, pennyroyal powder keeps pets free from fleas.

Pennyroyal's oldest medicinal use is to bring on delayed menstruation, and the oil is a powerful and dangerous abortefacient. Taken internally, the oil has proved fatal to a number of women who used it for unwanted pregnancies. Native Americans drank pennyroyal tea for cramping pains and, since the herb provokes sweating, to relieve colds. American pennyroyal has the same properties and uses.
Growing tips Propagate from cuttings or by root division. Plant out in rich, moist soil with some shade in summer. American pennyroyal is usually grown from seed and prefers a dry soil and a sunny position.
CAUTION Pennyroyal causes the muscles of the uterus to contract and should be avoided during pregnancy.

Pepper

Piper nigrum

Black pepper

Habitat Native to South India and the East Indies. Found in tropical forests and requires shade and high levels of humidity. Introduced and cultivated commercially in India, Indonesia, Sri Lanka, Brazil, and the West Indies. Often grown alongside other crops in plantations, e.g. coffee.

Description Perennial climbing vine with strong, woody stems that can reach 8m (20ft) but are usually pruned to 3m (10ft). At the joints of the branched stems are broad, glossy, dark green, oval leaves that are prominently veined and taper to a point. Small white flowers are followed by hanging clusters of round green or yellow berries that ripen to red.

Parts used: dried, unripe fruit.

History Pepper was once such a valuable commodity that ransoms were paid in it and the fortunes of the great Italian city of Venice were directly attributable to its trade in pepper. As late as the 15th century rents in England were commonly paid in pepper, as it was considered more stable than the currency of the time. This is the origin of the term 'peppercorn rent', which has come to mean a trivial amount.

Pepper's principal use is as a seasoning and condiment, but it also has digestive properties. It contains an alkaloid that stimulates the taste buds, and this in turn causes saliva and gastric juices to flow. Pepper has been employed medicinally for indigestion and flatulence, and also externally to encourage circulation. Aromatherapists use diluted essential oil of black pepper as a warming massage for painful muscles.

Periwinkle

Vinca major

Greater periwinkle

Habitat Native to Europe. Grows in woods, thickets and hedgerows on well-drained chalky and loamy soils. This is a familiar garden plant.

Description Perennial hedgerow plant with trailing or climbing stems from 30–90cm (1–3ft) that form a dense covering. The shiny, oval leaves are either blunt or sharply pointed, and are borne in pairs up the stem. From mid-spring to early summer attractive, purple-blue flowers appear with five, blunted triangular petals that resemble the blades of a fan. **Part used**: flowering plant.

History An old Italian name for the periwinkle is *fiore di morte*, flower of death, and it was once customary to lay periwinkle wreaths on the graves of dead babies. In England however, where the flower was known as sorcerer's violet, the periwinkle was a popular ingredient of charms and love potions. The French regard the colourful periwinkle as a symbol of friendship.

Medicinally, periwinkle is an astringent, healing herb. The fresh leaves were applied to wounds and inserted into the nostrils to stop nosebleeds. Herbalists recommend periwinkle infusions for heavy periods and also for bleeding gums. The Madagascar or Rosy Periwinkle *Catharanthus roseus*, a related species, is a traditional African folk remedy for diabetes. Research has uncovered its potential to inhibit cancer growth.

Growing tips Propagate from cuttings or from seed and plant in ordinary garden soil in a shady position. The stems can be invasive and may be employed as ground cover. The Madagascar Periwinkle may be grown in pots or outside as a bedding plant, but will not tolerate frost.

Peruvian Bark

Cinchona spp

Quinine tree, fever tree, Jesuits' bark

Habitat Cinchona is native to the Andes in tropical America, especially Peru and Ecuador. Also grown in India, East Africa, Burma, Sri Lanka, and Java.

Description Evergreen tree from 6–25m (20–83ft) that grows in mountainous regions, becoming shrubby at very high altitudes. The variable leaves are usually elliptical to oval and pointed, and are bright green in colour. They are veined with prominent midribs. The lilac-like flowers are very fragrant and deep rose-red, and in the species used medicinally, the corolla is ringed with hairs. **Part used**: dried bark.

History Native South Americans took Peruvian bark for fevers and passed their knowledge to the invading Spanish Conquistadors and their Jesuit priests. By 1677, the bark was officially listed in the *London Pharmacopeia*. Cinchona is the source of quinine, a valuable substance widely employed as an antimalarial agent in the tropics. Synthetic drug combinations have been introduced to protect against malaria but quinine remains effective in treating the disease.

Peruvian bark is still prescribed by herbalists for feverish conditions in general. The bark has a very bitter taste that stimulates the digestive juices and acts as a general tonic. Quinine water was once a popular beverage, usually mixed with gin.

CAUTION Peruvian bark should be avoided during pregnancy and used only as directed by a qualified practitioner.

Plantain

Plantago major

Greater plantain, rat's tail

Habitat Native to Europe; introduced and widespread in other temperate zones, including North America. Common on cultivated land, on roadsides and waste ground.
Description Common weed from 15–30cm (6–12in) with a basal rosette of blunted, oval, prominently-veined leaves. Distinctive, erect, cylindrical flower spikes appear from late spring to early autumn that are composed of tiny, purplish-green to yellowish-green flowers. **Parts used**: aerial parts.
History This tenacious weed was known to both Native Americans and Maoris as Englishman's foot, or White Man's foot, since it appeared to take root wherever white colonists settled. To the old Anglo-Saxon herbalists, plantain was a highly esteemed remedy for poisonous bites, while in parts of America the plant was known as snakeweed.

English herbalists once considered plantain indispensable for a wide range of ailments from fevers to ulcers, kidney problems and piles. The plant was also reputed to increase virility, probably on account of its phallic flowering spike. Plantain's oldest medicinal application is in the treatment of cuts, sores, bites and stings. The fresh leaves, which are rich in mucilage and astringent tannins, speed up the healing of wounds. The crushed leaves may be applied directly to ease painful bee stings, and are reputed to relieve the itching of poison-ivy rash. Plantain ointment is a traditional remedy for piles.

Pleurisy Root

Aesclepias tuberosa

Flux root, butterfly weed

Habitat Native to North America along the east coast, in the Appalachian region, and as far west as Arizona. Common in dry fields and along roadsides.

Description Attractive perennial to 60cm (2ft) with thick, hairy stems growing from a stout, knotty root. The alternate leaves are hairy, spear-shaped and deep green. From mid-summer to mid-autumn beautiful orange flowers appear in terminal umbels. **Part used**: root.

History The Appalachian Indians valued this root's expectorant properties, and it is a traditional remedy for chest complaints.

Poke Root

Phytolacca americana

Pokeweed, pigeon berry

Habitat Native North American plant from New England south to Florida and Texas. Naturalized all over Europe. Found on field edges, roadsides, and on cleared land.

Description Poisonous, bushy perennial on a thick, brown, branched root with green or purplish stems from 120–270cm (4–9ft). The oblong leaves taper to a point and give out an unpleasant smell. From late summer to mid autumn, white or purplish flowers appear at the ends of the stems, followed by clusters of round green berries that ripen to deep purple and resemble blackberries. **Part used**: dried root.

History This poisonous plant is a powerful purgative. Delaware Indians once considered it a remedy for rheumatism, and early settlers made ink from the ripe berries.

Pomegranate

Punica granatum

Habitat Native to Asia, particularly Iran, Afghanistan and the foothills of the Himalayas. Naturalized in warm, dry climates including the Mediterranean, Palestine, North Africa, and eastward to India and Pakistan. The fruits are cultivated commercially, and dwarf forms of the plant may be grown horticulturally in temperate regions.

Description Small deciduous tree or bush to 6m (20ft) with pale brown bark and slender branches with spines at the tips. The leaf buds and young shoots are red, and the opposite leaves are oval in shape, thick and glossy. Large, waxy, orange-red flowers are followed by the familiar reddish-yellow skinned fruits. These are the size of an orange with a tough, outer rind and many-seeded, pinkish-red pulp. **Parts used**: fruit and rind, root and bark.

History The pomegranate was mentioned in the Egyptian Ebers Papyrus, written about 2000 BC. Its striking red colour and many seeds made it an obvious fertility symbol, and it is reputedly the 'forbidden fruit' eaten by Eve in the Garden of Eden. In classical mythology, Persephone remained bound to Pluto after she ate a pomegranate in his underworld kingdom, Hades.

The medicinal qualities of the pomegranate were known to Pliny in the first century. He recommended the root bark for expelling tapeworms, for which it is an effective but nauseating remedy. In traditional Indian medicine, the bitter rind is used to treat dysentery, on account of its powerful astringency. The leaves have antibacterial properties and were once applied to sores.

Pomegranate juice is widely used in Middle Eastern cookery to flavour meat dishes, and it is the basis of the liqueur *Grenadine*.

Poppy, White

Papaver somniferum

Opium poppy

Habitat Native to the Middle East, also western Asia and south-east Europe. Naturalized in other parts of Europe and may be found wild on waste ground as an escape. Widely cultivated in South-east Asia, principally as a source of opium.

Description Annual with rigid pale green stems, usually with a few bristles on the flowering stalks. The leaves are oval to heart-shaped with coarsely indented margins and are pale greyish to bluish green. From mid- to late summer large, four-petalled delicate flowers appear that are usually white or bluish white, often with a purple blotch at the base of each petal. These are followed by oval green seed capsules, ringed at the base, and with a flattened top surmounted by a disk. They contain tiny, blue-grey seeds. **Parts used**: seed heads.

History Records concerning the use of the opium poppy date back 5000 years to the time of the ancient Sumerian civilization. Opium, the valuable substance produced exclusively by this species of poppy, is a thick, milky latex that is extracted from the unripe seed heads. It contains around 25 different alkaloids, notably morphine and codeine, which are powerful pain killers.

Medicinally, the opium poppy is valuable for its pain-killing, sedative, antispasmodic and expectorant properties. An opium-based cough syrup was developed in the 8th century, and a tincture of opium known as laudanum was a popular tranquillizer in Victorian times. Opium smoking inspired many artists and writers, and the poppy is the source of heroin, a morphine derivative. The ripe seeds contain no narcotic alkaloids and are used in baking.

Prickly Ash

Zanthoxylum americanum

Toothache tree

Habitat Native to North America from Canada south to
Nebraska and Virginia. This plant is found in wooded areas
on rich, moist soils.

Description Shrub or small tree to 3m (10ft) with sharp
spines on the branchlets and leaf stalks. In early spring, small
yellow-green flowers appear in the axils before the leaves. The
oval, pinnate leaves are arranged in groups of five to eleven.
They are dark green with a pleasant lemon scent and have soft
hairs on the undersides. Inky blue berries, surrounded by a
grey shell, grow in clusters on top of the branches. **Parts
used**: bark and berries.

History Prickly ash bark is a Native American remedy for
toothache and rheumatic pain, adopted by white settlers in the
19th century and introduced into American medicine in 1849.
Both the bark and berries act as stimulants, with both local
and general effects. Chewing the bark or taking it in powdered
form was once a popular remedy for toothache, reflected in
the name toothache tree. The bark appears to have functioned
as a counter-irritant rather than a pain-killer: the local
irritation probably served to distract the sufferer's attention
from the painful tooth. Prickly ash bark
and berries stimulate the digestion and
circulation. Herbalists may prescribe
them internally for a weak
digestion or colic. Externally
prickly ash acts as a local
stimulant and is helpful
for problems related to poor
circulation, such as cramp
and chilblains. The tree has
sustained its folk reputation
as a remedy for
rheumatism.

Pumpkin

Cucurbita pepo

Habitat Probably native to the eastern Mediterranean. Widely cultivated in warm and temperate climates, including the USA and Britain.

Description Trailing annual vine with long, branched stems to 6m (20ft) bearing large, rough, triangular, lobed leaves similar to those of the squashes. From early to mid-summer, attractive funnel-shaped, deep yellow flowers appear, and the flowering stalks swell and ripen into the familiar, bright orange, ribbed fruit that may weigh as much as 12kg (25lb).

Parts used: seeds.

History The pumpkin is an ancient food plant and fragments have been found in archeological excavations in Mexico that date back 4000 years. Pumpkins were once known as English melons, and the name is a corruption of the plant's old English name 'pompion'. As a vegetable, the pumpkin was much more popular with the English during the 17th century when pumpkin pie with apple was a traditional dish. In the USA, where the pumpkin has never lost its popularity, pumpkin pie is traditionally served at Thanksgiving. Fresh pumpkin seeds, eaten on rising, are an old remedy for worms and tapeworms. They also contain significant quantities of zinc, which helps the body to release stored vitamin A, and may, therefore, be helpful for such skin problems as acne. Pumpkin seeds also contain a substance that has some similarities to the male hormone, androgen, and herbalists consider them helpful for easing prostate problems.

Purslane

Portulaca oleracea

Garden or green purslane, pigweed

Habitat Developed from the wild variety that probably originated in the Middle East. Widespread in temperate and sub-tropical zones from China west to Europe. Naturalized in North and South America and also found in Britain.

Description Sprawling annual with fleshy stems to 15–30cm (6–12in) that are tinged with pink. The thick, succulent leaves grow in clusters and are bright green and spatulate. In late summer solitary or groups of two to three small yellow flowers appear, blooming only for a short period on sunny mornings.

Part used: fresh plant.

History Fresh purslane has been a popular salad herb in India and the Middle East for centuries. The garden variety did not appear at English tables until Elizabethan times, when the fleshy leaves were eaten in summer salads or served pickled in winter. Young purslane stems may be cooked and eaten like asparagus, and the sharp-tasting leaves added sparingly to salads.

Gerard considered purslane a valuable cooling remedy for fevers, while Culpeper prescribed the herb for gout. The leaves are a rich source of vitamin C and were later employed in the prevention of scurvy. Purslane tea is a diuretic and was drunk as a tonic. Today the herb is rarely used medicinally.

Growing tips Sow seed in spring in light, well-drained soil. Plant out seedlings 15cm (6in) apart in a sunny, sheltered position and water well. The leaves are ready for harvesting after 6–8 weeks.

Pyrethrum

COMPOSITAE

Chrysanthemum cinerariifolium

Habitat Native to coastal areas of Yugoslavia and its islands. Prefers chalky or pebbly shores but is also found inland on dry, stony hillsides. Cultivated commercially in Japan, South Africa, and California for use as a garden insecticide.

Description Tall perennial from 30–75cm (12–30in) with slender, hairy stems and dark green leaves that are deeply incised and divided into seven segments. From early summer to early autumn, solitary, white daisy-like flowers appear.

Parts used: dried flower heads.

History The dried, daisy-like flowers, first used by the Persians, eradicate garden pests such as aphids and ants.

Quassia

SIMARUBACEAE

Picrasma excelsa or *Picraena excelsa*

Bitter ash

Habitat Native to the West Indies; also found in tropical South America. Grows wild on plains and low mountain slopes.

Description Tree that resembles the ash to 20m (65ft) with smooth, greyish bark. The pinnate leaves are oblong and pointed at both ends, and from late autumn inconspicuous yellowish-green flowers appear. These are followed by shiny black berries the size of a pea. **Part used**: stem wood, without the bark.

History Bitter quassia bark was once taken to expel worms. An infusion of the chips effectively controls aphids.

Raspberry

Rubus idaeus

European wild raspberry

Habitat Native to Europe and Asia. Introduced elsewhere. Found in woodland clearings, on wood edges, railway embankments and heathland. Prefers moist, nutrient-rich soil and grows at altitudes of up to 2000m (6500ft). Cultivated garden varieties have been bred from this wild species.
Description Shrub with perennial roots and biennial, woody stems to 1.5m (5ft) that usually have prickles but occasionally lack them entirely. The oval leaves have markedly serrated edges and are arranged in groups of three or seven. The underside is downy. From spring to summer in the second year, clusters of small, white flowers appear in the upper axils. They are followed by the familiar, fragrant, cone-shaped clusters of soft red berries. **Parts used**: leaf and fruit.
History Wild raspberries have been picked and eaten since prehistoric times. Today, cultivated varieties are still made into jams, jellies, and liqueurs such as *Framboise*. Home-made raspberry vinegar, now exclusively used in cooking, was once taken for fevers and sore throats.

The leaf is the most valuable medicinal part of the raspberry and a tea is traditionally drunk by expectant mothers during the last three months of pregnancy to strengthen the uterus and to ease painful contractions during labour. The gentle astringency of raspberry leaves is also helpful for diarrhoea in children, and an infusion makes a good mouthwash for ulcers and bleeding gums.

R. strigosus, the North American wild red raspberry, has similar medicinal properties and uses.
Growing tips Cultivated varieties are propagated from root cuttings and then planted out in rich, loamy soil with canes for support.

Rosemary
Rosemarinus officinalis

Habitat Native to the Mediterranean and widely cultivated in temperate climates as a garden plant. Fragrant rosemary grows wild on rocky Mediterranean hillsides near the sea and prefers light, dry, chalky soils.

Description Very aromatic evergreen shrub to 1.5m (5ft) with numerous branches that are downy when young and later become woody with greyish-brown, scaly bark. The narrow, leathery leaves are spiky, with a dark green upper surface and a pale grey, downy underside. When rubbed they give off a strong fresh scent reminiscent of both camphor and pine. From spring to early summer two-lipped, pale blue flowers grow in clusters towards the ends of the branches. **Parts used**: leaves and oil.

History During exams, Greek students wore rosemary in their hair to aid their memories. Later, fresh sprigs were tossed into the grave at funerals – a sign that the deceased would always be remembered. Rosemary also symbolized fidelity and Anne of Cleves wore a rosemary wreath when she embarked on her ill-fated marriage to Henry VIII.

Rosemary's connection with the head persists since herbalists still recommend the herb for headaches and the oil, which stimulates the scalp, is commonly found in hair tonics and shampoos. Rosemary oil, too, is an old remedy for gout and muscular aches and pains. It was the active ingredient of the celebrated Hungary Water that restored movement to Queen Elizabeth of Hungary's paralysed limbs.

In the kitchen, rosemary is traditionally served with roast lamb.

Growing tips Propagate from cuttings taken in summer that have had time to develop roots. Plant out in a sheltered, sunny position in well-drained, chalky soil and protect from frost during the winter.

Rowan

ROSACEAE

Sorbus acuparia

Mountain ash

Habitat Native to northern Europe. Grows in deciduous forests, on moors, heaths, and rocky slopes. May be found at altitudes of over 1000m (3250ft) and is common in areas with high precipitation. Planted in towns, parks and gardens.
Description Deciduous tree to 10m (30ft) with smooth, shiny grey to greyish-brown bark. Although not related to the ash, the leaves are similar: usually with six or seven pairs. From spring to early summer, small, creamy white flowers appear in flat-topped umbels, and are followed by green, pea-sized berries that quickly ripen into attractive, bright orange-red berries. In autumn, the leaves, too, turn a bright scarlet.
Part used: fruit.
History Many old superstitions surround the rowan tree. In rural areas, it was customary on the eve of May Day to tie bunches of rowan twigs over barn doors to protect livestock from evil spirits. Wearing a necklace of rowan berries was said to keep a farmer's wife safe from the influence of witches.

Rowan berries are astringent and rather acidic. The juice has been used medicinally as a gargle for sore throats and laryngitis, and its astringency was useful in treating haemorrhoids. The fruit contains vitamin C and was formerly employed in the prevention of scurvy. Rowan jelly is a good substitute for cranberry sauce, and in the north of England, the berries were added to meat dishes. Northern Europeans fermented the berries to make a strong spirit, while rowanberry ale was once drunk in Wales.

Rue

Ruta graveolens

Herb of grace

Habitat Native to southern Europe and North Africa. This aromatic plant grows in hilly regions on poor, dry, rocky ground in sheltered situations. Widely cultivated in temperate climates, including Britain and North America, where it is also found wild as an escape.

Description Hardy, shrubby perennial to 60cm (24in). The lower stems are woody and bear alternate bluish-green leaves that are deeply sub-divided into small, spatulate leaflets. The leaves have a curious, pungent smell and a bitter taste. From summer to early autumn, yellowish-green flowers with four toothed petals grow in loose clusters towards the ends of the stems. **Part used**: leaves.

History Rue has been considered a powerful defence against poisoning, spells and witchcraft since the earliest times. The herb's reputation as a poison antidote was still being upheld by Elizabethan herbalist Gerard, who maintained that it would antidote every possible kind of poison, from snakebites to scorpion stings. Later still, judges carried rue to protect them from contagious 'jail fever'. Sprigs of the herb acted as sprinklers for holy water before High Mass, and rue came to symbolize the grace that follows repentance.

Rue has a long association with the eyes. Artists and crafts people ate rue to sharpen their eyesight, and monks copying out manuscripts took the herb to ease eyestrain. Today herbalists still recommend small doses of the herb for strained eyes and associated headaches. Externally, rue is thought to be helpful for rheumatic pains and homeopaths prescribe it for bone injuries like sprained wrists and ankles.

Growing tips Sow seed in late spring and transplant seedlings to a sheltered, sunny position. Rue prefers well-drained, chalky soil.

Saffron

Crocus sativus

Saffron crocus

Habitat Native to Asia Minor but now unknown in the wild. Widely cultivated in temperate regions, particularly Spain and France, also India and China. Grown horticulturally. Not to be confused with the wild and poisonous meadow saffron.
Description Typical crocus that is perennial and has no stem. In spring grass-like leaves rise directly from the corm and are greyish-green with sheathed bases. From early autumn, fragrant mauve, purple or reddish-purple six-petalled flowers appear. They have three distinctive orange-red stigmas and long yellow anthers. **Part used**: dried stigmas.
History The saffron crocus is represented in Cretan art dating back to 1600 BC. The dried stigmas yield an orange dye that has long been an important and costly item of trade. Eastern kings and holy men wore robes dyed with saffron, and both colour and fragrance were highly prized by the ancient Greeks and Chinese. The Arabs introduced saffron cultivation into Spain during the 10th century and from the 14th to the early 20th century, English saffron growing centred on the Essex town of Saffron Walden. Saffron was a popular medieval hair dye and was once considered an aphrodisiac.

Saffron is a fragrant and very expensive spice. Turmeric is often substituted, but purists consider saffron essential for such classic dishes as *paella*. In England, yellow saffron cakes are a traditional Cornish speciality.
Growing tips Plant corms in a rich, sandy soil in autumn at a depth of 10cm (4in) and at 15cm (6in) intervals. Choose a sheltered spot and protect from frost.

Sage

Salvia officinalis

Garden sage, narrow-leaved sage

Habitat Native to the northern Mediterranean coast,
particularly Yugoslavia where it is found wild in the hills.
Prefers poor, dry limestone soils in sunny situations. Over 750
species of sage are widely cultivated throughout the world in
temperate zones, and as far north as Canada.

Description Hardy, shrubby, branching perennial from 30–
70cm (12–30in) that is strongly aromatic. The young stems
are covered with a white down but become woody at the base
as they age. The surface of the thick, velvety leaves is
puckered and veined, and the underside is hairy. The leaves
are greyish-green, and oblong with rounded ends. From early
to mid-summer whorls of tubular, two-lipped, violet blue
flowers appear at intervals towards the ends of the stems.

Parts used: leaves and oil.

History The botanical name of the sage genus *Salvia* is from
the Latin verb *salvere* meaning to save, and refers to its
considerable medical reputation in ancient times. Sage was so
highly esteemed that by the 10th century it had acquired the
reputation of conferring immortality, an exaggerated claim
that persisted well into the
17th century.

   Sage tea was once as
popular as Indian tea and
the Chinese, who
considered it a digestive
tonic with calming
properties, traded it for
their own tea. Sage
tea may be taken
for anxiety
or sleeplessness, but its
oldest medicinal use
is for soothing
sore throats and
mouth
infections, on
account of its
antiseptic
and
antibacterial properties. Fresh
sage leaves rubbed on the teeth will deodorize the

mouth and strengthen the gums. This versatile herb has also been of cosmetic value since Roman times when a strong infusion of the herb was a popular hair darkener.

In Europe sage is a familiar kitchen herb. The fresh leaves complement cheese and onions, and the more pungent flavour of the dried herb goes well with veal and poultry.

Red Sage (*S. officinalis purpurea*) is a variant of garden sage that has purple-red foliage and grows to 45cm (18in). It is propagated by cuttings or by layering since the seeds usually revert to the green-leaved type. Red sage is considered particularly effective for sore throats, bleeding gums and mouth ulcers.

Clary Sage (*S. sclarea*) grows to 1m (3ft) and has large, oblong leaves with toothed margins that are dull green in colour and wrinkled. The herb is known as 'clear eye' on account of the medicinal value of the mucilaginous seeds. After they had been soaked in water, the liquid was used to clear the eyes of grit and other foreign bodies. The leaves, together with elderflowers, were used to flavour German wines and the German name for the herb was *muskateller*. Clary sage's balsamic-scented oil is used in perfumery.

Growing tips Sow seed in late spring or, for use the same year, propagate by layering or from cuttings. Sage prefers a well-drained soil and a sunny, sheltered position. Prune well in spring and renew woody plants every three to four years.

St John's Wort

Hypericum perforatum

Common St John's wort

Habitat Native to Europe and western Asia. Naturalized in North America, especially along the East Coast. Grows in open woods, meadows, hedgerows, grassy banks and roadsides, on dry, gravelly soils.

Description Spreading, aromatic, hardy perennial with long runners and an erect stem, branching at the top, that grows to 60cm (2ft). The round stem has two raised ridges running up its length. The pale-green leaves are small and oblong and are dotted with translucent oil glands. From late summer to mid-autumn clusters of five-petalled yellow flowers appear at the ends of the stems and are marked with small black oil glands. The whole plant gives off a heady, incense-like scent.

Part used: flowering plant.

History The history of St John's Wort has long been bound up with mysticism. In pre-Christian times sprays of the fragrant plant were suspended over ikons to drive away evil spirits. Later, the herb became associated with John the Baptist. When crushed, the red pigment in the flower petals stains them red and the plant was reputed to 'bleed' on the anniversary of the Saint's beheading.

To the early herbalists, it was clear from St John's Wort's blood-like juice that the herb would be an effective wound-healer. It was used to dress sword cuts in the Middle Ages and afterwards for wounds, ulcers, and burns. Modern analysis attributes the herb's qualities to its antibacterial and astringent properties.

Growing tips Propagate from seed, from cuttings, or by root division. St John's Wort will flourish in ordinary garden soil and prefers a sunny position, but with some shade.

Sarsaparilla

Smilax officinalis and spp.

Honduras sarsaparilla, red sarsaparilla

Habitat Native to Central America and found in the tropical Amazonian rain forests, in swamps and on river banks.
Description Climbing or trailing vine with arrow-shaped, veined leaves and woody stems that rise from a long, tuberous, knotted rootstock. The stems bear sharp prickles and climb by means of tendrils. The small, greenish to white flowers grow in umbels from the leaf axils. **Part used**: root.
History This 16th-century cure for syphilis is now considered beneficial for skin complaints and rheumatism.

Sassafras

LAURACEAE

Sassafras albidum

Habitat Native to eastern North America from Michigan southwards to Florida and eastwards to Texas. Grows on wood edges and waysides on sandy soils.
Description Aromatic deciduous tree to around 9m (30ft) with rough, greyish, fissured bark. In spring, before the leaves have formed, clusters of pale yellow-green flowers appear. The alternate leaves are usually three-lobed, with downy undersides. The fruits are pea-sized, dark blue berries. Both the bark and the leaves have a refreshing fennel-like fragrance. **Parts used**: bark and root bark.
History Native Americans once took sassafras root for fevers. Externally, the antiseptic root bark heals sores and eases poison-ivy rash.

Saw Palmetto

Serenoa serrulata

Habitat Native to North America along the Atlantic coast
from Texas through Florida northwards to South Carolina.
Grows in dense patches on swampy, low-lying coastal plains.
Description Low, shrubby palm from 1–2m (3–6ft) with
creeping underground stems that produce a crown of green
palm-like leaves that are often coated with white and have
sharp, saw-toothed stalks. Inconspicuous flowers appear in
clusters followed in autumn by berries that resemble black
olives when ripe. **Part used**: fruit.
History Native Americans collected the ripe fruits of the saw
palmetto for food and considered them both nutritious and a
digestive tonic. The fattening berries were thought to increase
male virility and so were taken raw or ground up as an
aphrodisiac. Scientific analysis has confirmed the presence of
steroidal components in the berries, and these are thought to
be responsible for the herb's tonic effect on the male
reproductive system. Herbalists recommend the berries for an
enlarged prostate gland and
they have also been used to
treat impotence. Saw
palmetto has soothing
and expectorant
properties, which
explains why a
tea of the
berries is
traditionally
taken
for bronchitis
and
catarrhal
complaints.

Self Heal

Prunella vulgaris

Heal-all, carpenters' herb, woundwort

Habitat Native to Europe, North America and Asia and introduced elsewhere. Common in meadows, grassland and open woodland, on moist soils in sunny situations.
Description Perennial on square, grooved stem to 20cm (8in) that may be erect or low-growing. Pairs of opposite, hairy leaves are spaced regularly up the stem and are oblong to ovate. Compact spikes of lipped, violet flowers appear from mid-summer to early autumn at the tips of the stems with a pair of stalkless leaves directly beneath, like a collar. **Part used**: flowering plant.
History Self-heal's easy availability and its medicinal properties ensured its reputation as a domestic wound-healer. Gerard sang self-heal's praises claiming that 'there is not a better Wound herbe in the world than Self-Heale', while Culpeper called it 'an especial herb for inward or outward wounds'. To exponents of the Doctrine of Signatures, the tubular, deep-red flowers resembled an inflamed throat and the plant was designated a remedy for such throat diseases as quinsy. Indeed, the botanical name of the plant *Prunella*, originally *Brunella,* is derived from the German for quinsy, *die Braune.*

Self-heal is an astringent and antiseptic herb which, in strong infusion, helps to check the flow of blood. Herbalists still consider a poultice of the fresh leaves helpful for healing cuts and wounds, while an infusion makes an effective mouthwash for mouth and throat infections.

Senna

Cassia senna

Alexandrian senna

Habitat Native to North Africa, Egypt, Sudan and Jordan. Indian senna *c. angustifolia* is native to southern India.
Description Perennial shrub to 60cm (2ft) with pale green, erect stems and spreading branches. The leaves are grouped in four to five pairs and are lance-shaped, brittle in texture, and greyish green. Erect spikes of small, five-petalled yellow flowers are followed by oblong pods containing about six seeds. **Part used**: dried pods.
History Senna was known to Arabic physicians as early as the 9th century, and the name itself is of Arabic origin. Both the pods and the leaves of the shrub have a powerful purgative action, but the milder pods are preferred and are a long-established remedy for constipation. Senna's active constituents, which are similar to those of rhubarb, are bowel irritants and stimulants. Taking senna, however, can result in griping pains and feelings of nausea. For this reason, it is traditionally combined with spices that calm the digestive system, such as ginger or cloves. Herbalists advise against the long-term use of senna pods since the intestinal muscles, which would normally control evacuation, can lose their tone and function. The body then becomes dependent on laxatives.

CAUTION
Chronic constipation
requires medical attention.

Shepherd's Purse

Capsella bursa-pastoris

Pepper and salt

Habitat Native to Europe and established worldwide in temperate zones. A common weed found in fields, gardens, roadsides and waste ground.

Description Annual with a basal rosette of grey-green, dandelion-like leaves and slender stems that are sparsely branched. The smaller stem leaves are arrow-shaped. Small, white inconspicuous flowers bloom for most of the year at the end of the flowering stems, and are followed by flattened triangular seed pods. **Part used**: fresh or dried plant.

History This common plant acquired its name on account of its curious, pouch-shaped seed pods. These resemble the old type of leather purse that was commonly worn on a belt around the waist, although not exclusively by shepherds.

The herb is an old domestic remedy that is very effective for stopping internal and external bleeding. Culpeper prescribed an ointment of the fresh leaves for wounds, while for nose bleeds, a cotton-wool ball saturated with the juice was inserted into the nostrils. Internally, an infusion of the herb was drunk for diarrhoea and stomach ulcers. During World War I the Germans used an extract of shepherd's purse for staunching wounds. Herbalists continue to recommend shepherd's purse for wounds and varicose veins, while an infusion is considered helpful for excessively heavy periods.

The young leaves have a very sharp, cress-like flavour and were eaten as a vegetable, hence the country name, pepper and salt.

Skullcap

Scutellaria latifolia and spp.

Mad-dog weed

Habitat Native to Canada and northern and eastern USA. Grows in wet meadows and near rivers and lakes. A related species *S. galericulata* is found in Britain.

Description Perennial with square, slender stems from 15–45cm (6–18in) and opposite, ovate leaves with serrated edges that taper to a point. From mid-summer to early autumn pairs of two-lipped, pouched, bright blue flowers bloom in the leaf axils.

Part used: dried plant.

History Mad-dog weed reflects skullcap's old use as a remedy for rabid-dog bites. It is also said to ease headaches.

Skunk Cabbage

Symplocarpus foetidus

Habitat Native to swampy areas of the eastern USA and westwards to Iowa.

Description Perennial with tuberous, fleshy rootstock that sends up a sheathed, fleshy, oval spike that bears small, purple flowers from late winter to early spring, before the leaves appear. The plant grows to 40cm (16in) and bears heart-shaped, thick-stalked leaves that resemble those of the cabbage. The whole plant gives off a foetid, unpleasant smell. **Part used**: rootstock.

History This foul-smelling plant has expectorant properties and a mild sedative action. Both are helpful for coughing spasms.

Slippery Elm

Ulmus fulva

Indian elm, moose elm

Habitat Native North American tree growing in moist woods and along streams from southern Canada southwards to Florida and Texas. Also grown as an ornamental.

Description Deciduous tree to 15m (50ft) with ridged, dark brown bark and whitish, aromatic inner bark. The leaf buds are covered in thick yellowish felt. The alternate, roughish, leaves are dark green and oblong to obovate with serrated edges. Dense clusters of inconspicuous flowers without stalks appear in spring. **Part used**: inner bark.

History Slippery elm bark is an old-established Native American remedy, hence the tree's common name, Indian elm. A tea of the moist inner bark was taken for digestive problems, particularly diarrhoea, since it is rich in a soothing mucilage. Slippery elm bark swells in water to make a soothing and nourishing food and herbalists consider it one of the best remedies for healing inflammations of the gastro-intestinal tract. The powdered bark, commonly known as slippery elm food, may be sold commercially as a nourishing drink for convalescents and those recovering from gastro-intestinal illnesses.

Commercial collection of the inner bark in spring can lead to permanent damage or destruction of the tree. Consequently, and especially after taking into account the harmful effects of Dutch elm disease, the slippery elm is becoming less common in the wild and supplies of the inner bark are limited.

Soapwort

CARYOPHYLLACEAE

Saponaria officinalis

Fullers' herb, latherwort

Habitat Native to western Asia. Naturalized in Europe and eastern North America. Common on roadsides, railway embankments, and waste ground.

Description Perennial with a single, thick, slightly branched stem to 80cm (32in), and oval leaves that clasp the stem and narrow to a point. From mid-summer to early autumn clusters of large pale pink flowers with five petals and ten stamens grow at the top of the stem. **Parts used**: fresh stems and root.

History Soapwort root and stems are rich in saponins which, when boiled in water, yield a gentle lather. During the Middle Ages, the plant was commonly grown around wool mills, and the soapy liquid it produced was extensively employed to de-grease and thicken woollen cloth, a method known as 'fulling'. Soapwort's gentle action is ideal for cleaning tapestries, and for old and delicate fabrics that would not survive washing in detergent-based products. For a mild soap or shampoo, soak and boil the dried root, or boil the fresh stems.

Soapwort's lather-forming components irritate the digestive tract and the herb is a powerful purgative. Some herbalists have prescribed small doses of the herb as a laxative but others consider it unsafe for internal use. Externally, a soapwort solution is a traditional remedy for itchy skin conditions.

Growing tips Soapwort self-seeds and is easy to grow. It prefers moist, loamy soil and a sunny position.

Solomon's Seal

Polygonatum multiflorum

Sealwort, dropberry

Habitat Native to northern Europe and eastwards to Siberia and Asia. Naturalized in eastern North America. Grows wild in woods and shady places. Also cultivated as a garden plant.
Description Perennial, closely related to lily of the valley, with a thick, jointed, horizontal rootstock that bears circular scars. The erect stem inclines towards the tip and grows to 60cm (2ft). The leaves are elliptic, dark green and marked with numerous parallel veins. From spring to early summer drooping clusters of tubular, greenish-white, fragrant flowers appear that grow to one side. **Part used**: rootstock.
History The common name of this old-fashioned garden flower either refers to the scars on the rootstock, which were likened to the impression of a seal, or to the appearance of markings resembling Hebrew characters on a cross-section of the cut root. According to the Elizabethan herbalist Gerard, the plant also acquired its name on account of the root's ability to seal or heal up broken bones and he also prescribed it for 'any bruises, blacke or blew spots gotten by fals or by women's wilfulness in stumbling upon their hastie husband's fists'.

Solomon's seal root has soothing, tonic and astringent properties and Culpeper tells us that 17th-century Italian ladies employed the distilled root-water to clear the complexion of freckles and blemishes. Externally, poultices of the bruised root were applied to bruises and inflammations.
Growing tips Sow seed in autumn or propagate by root division. Solomon's seal is a hardy plant that prefers light garden soil and a shady position.

Sorrel

Rumex acetosa and spp.

Common sorrel, sour sauce

Habitat Native to Europe, particularly Britain. Introduced and naturalized in North America. Grows wild in meadows and grassland, along roadsides, and in open woods.

Description Perennial member of the dock family with slender green stems that may be tinged with red from 40–100cm (20–39in). The thick, tapering, dark green leaves resemble spinach. They are arrow-shaped at the base with rounded lobes, and become smaller and oblong towards the top of the stalk. Small, reddish-brown or reddish-green flowers grow in thin spikes from early to late summer and they have conspicuous veins. Common sorrel is closely related to the cultivated French sorrel *R. scutatus*, which has fleshier, more heart-shaped leaves. **Part used**: leaves.

History Sorrel, from the old French for sour, is well known for its acidity. The leaves make excellent soups and fish sauces, and have been used in cooking since the time of the ancient Egyptians. The Romans served sorrel to balance their rich food and old English recipes recommend sour green sorrel sauce with pork and goose.

Sorrel leaves were traditionally made into a cooling drink for feverish conditions and poultices were recommended for skin problems. Fresh sorrel contains vitamin C and was once taken as a preventive against scurvy.

Growing tips Sow seed in mid-spring in a rich soil in a sunny, preferably sheltered position. The leaves may be harvested after about four months.

CAUTION Large doses of sorrel may damage the kidneys. Avoid sorrel if you suffer from kidney disease, arthritis or rheumatism.

Southernwood

Artemisia abrotanum

Lad's love, *Garde-robe*

Habitat Native to southern Europe, especially Spain and Italy. Naturalized in temperate zones, including the eastern USA. Grown as a garden ornamental but may not flower in cooler, northern climates.

Description Strong, sharp-smelling bushy perennial and member of the wormwood family. The branching stems grow from 90–150cm (3–5ft) and bear grey-brown, often downy leaves that are finely divided and feathery. Loose clusters of small, inconspicuous, yellowish-white flowers appear from late summer to early autumn. **Parts used**: whole plant.

History In rural areas, where southernwood was known as lad's love and maid's ruin, the herb acquired a reputation for increasing young men's virility. It was popularly employed in love potions and adolescent boys even rubbed an ointment on their cheeks to speed up the growth of facial hair.

The plant is related to the wormwoods and the volatile oil in the leaves is responsible for the strong, sharp, scent which repels moths and other insects. It was customary to lay sprays of the herb amongst clothes, or hang them in closets, and this is the origin of southernwood's French name, *garde-robe* (clothes-preserver). Judges carried posies of southernwood and rue to protect them from prisoners' contagious diseases, and some churchgoers relied on the herb's sharp scent to keep them awake during long sermons.

Growing tips Propagate by root division in spring or autumn and plant in a sunny position.

Squaw Vine

Mitchella repens

Partridgeberry

Habitat Native to North America
from Nova Scotia southwards
to Florida and Texas. Grows in
forests and woodland, around the
bottom of trees and tree stumps.
Description Trailing evergreen
with rooting stems up to 1m
(3ft) in length. The dark green
leaves are opposite and resemble
those of clover with shiny upper
surfaces. Tubular white flowers grow in
pairs from early to mid-summer and
are followed by a scarlet, many-seeded
berry. **Parts use**: flowering plant.
History Squaw vine tea is a traditional Native American
remedy for facilitating childbirth.

Stone Root

Collinsonia canadensis

Horseweed

Habitat Native to North America from
Quebec westwards to
Wisconsin and southwards
to Florida. This plant is
found in moist woods.
Description Unpleasant
smelling perennial. The hard,
brownish-grey, knobbly rhizome
sends up a four-sided stem from 30–120cm
(1–4ft) with opposite, ovate leaves
that are heart-shaped at the base
and have serrated edges. From J
uly to September large,
two-lipped greenish-yellow flowers
grow in a loose terminal spike. **Parts used**: root and rhizome.
History The root is a traditional remedy for urinary stones,
while horseweed reflects its former use in veterinary medicine.

Summer Savory

Satureia hortensis

Habitat Native to the Mediterranean and introduced to Britain and North America. Savory is widely cultivated as a culinary herb.

Description Very aromatic annual from 30–45cm (12–18in). The erect, branching stems are covered with fine hairs and bear pairs of oblong, pointed leaves with a purplish tinge. Small, two-lipped white to rose pink flowers bloom in groups of three to six in the upper leaf axils from late summer to mid-autumn. Winter savory (*S. montana*), a hardy perennial, is bushier, woody at the base. It has a stronger scent than summer savory but its flavour is considered inferior. **Parts used**: leaves and flowering tops.

History In Europe, the leaves of both summer and winter savory were a traditional flavouring for food long before the arrival of Eastern spices. The Romans brought the herb to England and the Saxons named it savory, after its biting, thyme-like flavour. In the 17th century, fish and meat were coated in breadcrumbs seasoned with savory, and today summer savory is used in stuffings and with roast meats. Savory eases flatulence and in Germany it is traditionally served with beans.

The genus *Satureia* means belonging to the satyrs. The savorys' association with these lascivious, mythological creatures probably accounts for their reputation as aphrodisiacs.

Growing tips Sow summer savory seeds in spring in a sunny position in ordinary garden soil. Thin out to 25cm (10in) and water well during hot, dry weather.

Sunflower

Helianthus annuus

Habitat Native to Central America, probably originating in Peru. Introduced and widely cultivated in North America, the Mediterranean, eastern Europe, and the USSR. Also grown as a garden ornamental.

Description Tall, striking annual with a stout, rough, hairy stem from 1–3m (3–10ft). The rough-textured leaves are broad with coarsely serrated edges and have prominent veins. The familiar bright yellow flowers have honeycomb-like brownish centres composed of small tubular flowers that ripen into the familiar pale-greyish seeds. **Parts used**: seed, seed oil.

History The round yellow heads of the sunflower resemble the sun's disk surrounded by rays, and the blossoms are said to rotate so that they always face the sun. In ancient Peru the sun-worshipping Incas saw in the sunflower the face of their sun god. Sunflower headdresses were worn by the Inca priestesses and flowers wrought in gold adorned Inca temples.

Sunflower seeds are rich in a mild, pale yellow oil that is popular for cooking and extensively used in margarines. It is considered healthier for the arteries than butter, due to its low saturated fat content. Sunflower seeds are also rich in the B vitamins. Herbalists once prescribed the expectorant and diuretic seeds for colds, coughs and bronchitis. The leaves and flowers, which have weak insecticidal properties, were formerly employed as a preventive against malaria.

Growing tips Sow seed in boxes under glass and transfer seedlings to pots. Harden off and plant out in deep, well-manured soil 60cm (2ft) apart with a tall stick for support. Choose a sunny position with shelter from strong winds.

Sweet Cicely

Myrrhis odorata

British myrrh, sweet fern, sweet chervil

Habitat Native to Europe, including northern Britain. Naturalized in North America. Found in grassy places, in hedgerows and on wood edges, often in hilly regions.

Description Perennial to 1m (3ft) with a strong, sweet scent, reminiscent of anise. The stout, branching stem is grooved and hairy, and bears large, aromatic, fern-like leaves that are bright green above and paler beneath. The leaves are subdivided into narrow, toothed leaflets, and the stem leaves are sheathed. From mid-spring to early summer, umbels of numerous white flowers appear, and are followed by large, brown, ridged seeds. **Part used**: leaves.

History Sweet cicely was a favourite cottage-garden herb in 17th-century England on account of its sweet-smelling, sugary leaves with their anise-like flavour. The herb is traditionally cooked with tart fruits, such as rhubarb and gooseberries, and added to fruit salads. The fresh leaves impart their own sweetness so less sugar is needed, and they also complement such root vegetables as parsnips. The seeds may be substituted for caraway in cakes and biscuits.

Sweet cicely root is mildly antiseptic and, steeped in brandy or wine, was a home remedy for consumption. A tea of the seeds also served as a digestive. As a medicinal herb, however, sweet cicely – 'so harmless you cannot use it amiss' – does not appear to have made much of an impression.

Growing tips
Sow seed in early spring or autumn or propagate by root division in autumn. Choose a shady position in moist, well-drained soil. Germination may be slow.

Sweet Violet

Viola odorata

VIOLACEAE

Habitat Native to Europe, North Africa, and Asia.
Introduced and naturalized in temperate zones, including
North America. Found in hedgerows, wood clearings and on
wood edges. Cultivated commercially.

Description Fragrant, low-growing perennial to 15cm (6in)
with dark green kidney- or heart-shaped leaves that grow on
long footstalks. The leaves are downy beneath and the edges
are scalloped. From early to mid-spring, pretty, sweet-scented,
drooping flowers bloom singly. They have five petals, the
lower one spurred, and the colour varies from deep purple to
lilac, pinkish-lilac, and even white. **Parts used**: leaves, flowers
and rootstock.

History The violet genus is reputedly named in honour of Io,
one of Zeus' many lovers. After she was turned into a white
heifer to escape the wrath of his wife, Hera, violets
materialized at her feet so that she would have enough to eat.
In the language of flowers, the violet signifies modesty as well
as fidelity, and posies of violets were reputedly exchanged
between Napoleon Bonaparte and Josephine.

The violet's historical reputation as a sedative
dates back to classical Greece when the
Athenians made a sleeping
potion from the flowers.
Gerard prescribed a syrup
of violets for insomnia,
headaches and sore
throats. Herbalists value
the violet's expectorant
and antiseptic properties
and recommend the leaves
and flowers for coughs,
bronchitis and catarrh.

Violets are edible and
the crystallized petals
make an attractive
decoration for cakes
and chocolates.
Violets are used to
colour and flavour
a French liqueur,
Parfait amour.

Tansy

Tanacetum vulgare

Buttons, bachelor's buttons

Habitat Native to Europe and Asia. Introduced and naturalized in north-eastern USA from Nova Scotia westwards to Minnesota and southwards to Missouri. Found in hedgerows, along roadsides and on waste ground.

Description Straggling perennial with erect, leafy stems from 60–90cm (2–3ft). The finely cut, alternate leaves are fern-like and the leaflets are deeply lobed or toothed. When brushed they give off a camphor-like smell. From mid-summer to early autumn, loose clusters of button-like flower heads appear that are an attractive golden yellow. **Part used**: flowering plant.

History Legend has it that Ganymede, the beautiful cupbearer to the Greek gods, drank a potion of tansy blossoms to secure his immortality. A more prosaic explanation for tansy's association with immortality is to be found in the plant's insecticidal and deodorizing properties. Sprigs of tansy were once laid over corpses to preserve them from decay, strewn over floors to mask unpleasant smells, and rubbed on joints of meat to repel flies.

In England young, sharp-tasting tansy leaves were traditionally made into Easter puddings and cakes. Tansy effectively expels worms from the body, and may have been beneficial after a Lenten diet of salted fish.

Culpeper regarded tansy as a fertility aid, as did Native Americans who used a poultice of the fresh leaves to encourage conception. Herbalists still consider small doses of tansy useful for expelling worms.

CAUTION In large doses, tansy brings on menstruation .

Tarragon

Artemisia dracunculus

French tarragon, 'true' French tarragon

Habitat Native to southern Europe. Introduced elsewhere as a garden herb and cultivated commercially in Europe, Asia, and the USA. Russian tarragon, *A. dracunculoides,* a closely related plant, is a native of Siberia and the Caspian Sea.

Description Bushy, aromatic perennial from 60–90cm (2–3ft) that resembles wormwood. The slender stems bear smooth, dark, shiny leaves. They are narrow and linear in shape and widely spaced along the stem. From mid- to late summer, small globular flowers appear that are greyish-green or greenish-white, and woolly. French tarragon will only flower in warm climates. Russian tarragon is a taller, coarser plant with roughish, pale green leaves. **Part used**: leaves.

History The Romans thought tarragon would ward off exhaustion and it was customary for Medieval pilgrims to start out with fresh sprigs inside their boots. The root was once a popular cure for toothache, and chewing the fresh leaves does have a mildly numbing effect.

Today, tarragon is no longer used medicinally. It is, however, one of the most important of European culinary herbs and is widely employed to flavour vinegar and mustard. It is also included in *fines herbes* mixtures and complements eggs and chicken. Russian tarragon's coarser, more pungent taste is considered inferior.

Growing tips 'True' French tarragon must be started from cuttings as the seed always produces the Russian variety. Plant out in spring in well-drained soil in a sunny, sheltered position. Protect from wind and frost during winter.

Thuja

Thuja occidentalis

Northern white cedar, Tree of life

Habitat Native to North America from Quebec southwards to North Carolina. Grows along the banks of streams and rivers, and in moist places. Introduced into Europe and Britain as an ornamental tree in gardens and parks.

Description Conifer that can reach 21m (70ft) but in the UK rarely exceeds 10m (30ft). The tree has a rather ragged conical crown, yet a graceful appearance. The trunk is covered in a light brown outer bark that is composed of long, flaking strips. The shortish branches bear opposite pairs of bright green, mildly fragrant leaves that are composed of overlapping scales. The surface is rough in texture due to raised glands on each leaf. Minute greenish-yellow flowers bloom at the tips of the branches from mid-spring to mid-summer and are followed by small pale green cones that ripen to light chestnut.

Parts used: young twigs.

History In pre-Christian times it was customary to burn sweet-scented thuja wood during sacrificial rites. The tree was introduced into France from Canada and planted in the grounds of the royal palace at Fontainebleau.

Thuja's active principle, a volatile oil called thujone, acts on the muscles of the uterus and Native Americans drank a tea of the inner bark to promote menstruation. Thuja also tones the bronchial passages and herbalists may prescribe it for bronchitis and catarrh. Externally, thuja is said to cure warts.

CAUTION
Thujone is toxic. Avoid during pregnancy and take only under professional direction.

Thyme

Thymus vulgaris

Common thyme, garden thyme

Habitat Native to the western Mediterranean and southern Italy where it may be found wild. Introduced elsewhere and widely cultivated, especially in Hungary and Germany.

Description Perennial that may be grown as an annual in cold climates. Bushy herb with several, many-branched, wooded stems that grows from 10–30cm (4–12in) with strongly aromatic leaves. These are small, narrow, and elliptical to lance-shaped with greyish-green uppers and downy undersides. From early to mid-summer, whorls of lilac to pink, tubular, lipped flowers grow in clusters at the tips of the branches. **Part used**: flowering plant.

History This herb's name may be derived from the Greek word for courage, or from a term meaning to fumigate. In the Age of Chivalry thyme motifs were embroidered on the scarves of jousting knights. Sprigs of the herb were thought to ward off the plague and were burned indoors to cleanse the air.

Thymol, thyme's essential oil, is strongly antibacterial, and it was used as an antiseptic during World War I. Thyme tea is a traditional remedy for digestive complaints and the herb's expectorant properties are helpful for irritable coughs. In the kitchen, thyme is an essential part of a *bouquet garni*, and it both flavours and extends the keeping qualities of sausages, meat loaf and stuffings.

Growing tips Sow seed indoors in the warmth, or propagate from cuttings. Plant out seedlings in a sunny, sheltered position in light, very well-drained soil. Thyme prefers poor, fairly rocky soil.

CAUTION Thyme oil is toxic and should not be taken internally.

Valerian

Valeriana officinalis

Common valerian, garden heliotrope

Habitat Native to Europe and western Asia. Naturalized in North America, from New England southwards to New Jersey. Found in rough meadowland, on moist grassland, along the banks of streams and ditches.

Description Tall, conspicuous, rather foetid smelling perennial from 90–120cm (3–4ft). The single, grooved stem is hairy towards the base, and bears slender horizontal branches and pairs of dark green, pinnate leaves. They are joined at the base and ovate to lance-shaped with uneven, ascending indentations. The upper surface of the leaves is veined and softly hairy. From early to late summer two or more pairs of flowering stems bear loose clusters of palest pink to white, five-petalled flowers that have a slight fragrance.

Part used: rootstock.

History In medieval times Valerian was considered a cure-all, and one suggested origin of its name is the Latin verb *valere* meaning to be well. The herb acquired a reputation as a cure for epilepsy, due to the valuable antispasmodic properties of the root, and it was extensively employed from the mid-16th century to treat convulsions and other nervous disorders. Valerian is a very effective natural tranquillizer and modern herbalists consider the herb a valuable remedy for nervous anxiety and insomnia. It has a particular reputation for calming pre-flight nerves.

Rat-catchers lured rats into their traps with the scent of valerian and the legendary Pied Piper probably carried valerian roots in his pockets. Cats also love the scent. The Anglo-Saxons ate valerian in salads.

Verbena, Lemon

VERBENACEAE

Aloysia triphylla

Habitat Native to Chile and Argentina, and widespread in tropical countries. Introduced into temperate zones, and cultivated commercially in France and North Africa. Commonly grown indoors in pots.

Description Lemon-scented, woody, deciduous shrub that reaches 3m (10ft) in warm climates, but rarely grows higher than 1.5m (5ft) in cooler countries. The rough-textured branches bear fragrant, narrow, lance-shaped leaves that are arranged in whorls of three. They are pale green with a prominent mid-rib and oil glands are visible on the undersides. From late summer slender spikes of numerous, tiny pale lavender flowers bloom towards the end of the branches. **Part used**: leaves.

History Spanish colonists, delighted by this lemon-scented shrub, brought it back to Europe from South America. Later, the essential oil was extracted and used in soaps and perfumery. The fragrance was once popular with ladies of the American Deep South.

Lemon verbena is usually encountered in the form of a delicate-flavoured tisane. Taken hot, its sedative properties are said to soothe frayed nerves, and it also acts as a digestive. The young leaves add a citrus tang to fruit drinks and fruit salads, and may be substituted for lemon rind in sweet sauces. The herb should be used sparingly: some people find the taste rather soapy.

Growing tips Propagate from cuttings taken in summer. Plant in a light, well-drained soil in a very sheltered, sunny position as the plant is easily damaged by cold and wind. Cut back in winter and cover the base with straw. In North America lemon verbena is usually grown indoors as a house plant.

Vervain

Verbena officinalis

Herb of grace, Holy herb, Enchanter's plant

Habitat Native to Europe, particularly the Mediterranean region, and naturalized in North America. Grows on roadsides, rough pastures and on waste ground. Prefers chalky soils.

Description Perennial with sparsely leaved, slender, angular stems from 30–90cm, (1–3ft). The oblong, ovate leaves are opposite and usually deeply lobed. The upper leaves clasp the stem and are covered in short hairs; the lower are stalked. Tiny white, lilac-tinged flowers appear at the tips of the long, flowering stalks throughout the summer months. They have five petals and no scent. **Part used**: flowering plant.

History Vervain, the enchanter's plant, has a long association with mysticism and magic. The Romans employed vervain as an altar plant, and the ancient Egyptians dedicated it to the sorceress-goddess Isis. In Celtic Britain, the Druids included the herb in the purifying or 'lustral' water they used for sacrifices. According to Christian legend, vervain stemmed the bleeding from Christ's wounds, which assured its reputation as a potent healer.

In Medieval times, people wore necklaces of the fresh plant for luck, and believed that vervain would protect them from headaches and snakebites. Modern herbalists also consider vervain helpful for headaches, particularly migraine-type headaches accompanied by nausea, and the herb is said to have a strengthening effect on the nervous system.

CAUTION Avoid during pregnancy.

Virginia Snakeroot

Aristolochia serpentaria

Serpentary, birthwort

Habitat Native to North America from the eastern and central USA southwards. Grows in shady woods.

Description Perennial with erect, wavy stems to 60cm (2ft) rising from a horizontal rhizome that sends out numerous slender roots. The foliage is rather sparse and composed of alternate, heart-shaped leaves that taper to a point. In early summer, dull purplish-brown, tubular flowers appear on short scaly stalks from the base of the stem, and may give off an unpleasant scent. The drooping flowers grow very low and can touch the ground. **Part used**: root.

History Virginia snakeroot once enjoyed a considerable reputation for curing rattlesnake and other poisonous bites and stings. According to some sources, early Egyptian snake charmers employed the roots of a related species to paralyze snakes. There is also a suggestion of snakes in the unusual, low-growing, S-shaped flowers. Native American Indian tribes applied the chewed root to snakebites, and early American settlers followed their example. Virginia snakeroot was introduced into European medicine from the mid-16th century and continued to be regarded as one of the foremost cures for snake bites up until the mid-18th century.

Today, virginia snakeroot is not widely employed medicinally as one of the active principles in the root, if taken in sufficient quantities, can result in intense vomiting attacks and damage to the internal organs.

Walnut

Juglans regia, Juglans nigra

Common walnut, English or Persian walnut, Black walnut

Habitat The common walnut *J. regia*, is probably native to Iran but extends westwards to the Balkan Mountains and eastwards to China. Introduced and found wild in open woodland in Europe, and southern and central England. Widely cultivated in warm climates, especially Spain. The black walnut *J. nigra* is native to the Appalachian Mountains of North America.

Description Deciduous tree from 25–30m (75–80ft) with spreading boughs and a wide crown. The massive trunk is deeply fissured and covered in smooth greyish slabs of bark. The very aromatic dull green, pinnate leaves have seven to nine leaflets. These are ovate, pointed at the tip, smooth-edged, with a prominent mid-rib. In spring drooping male catkins and inconspicuous female flowers appear, followed in autumn by globular green fruits that surround the light brown, wrinkled husk of the walnut. The black walnut has dark, ridged bark, and around fifteen leaflets with serrated edges.

Parts used: leaves and fruit.

History *Juglans* means Jupiter's acorn. In folk medicine the walnut is still associated with the philandering Jupiter: the green outer shell allegedly increases virility.

The ancient Romans extracted the brown stain from walnut husks and leaves for use as a hair dye, a practice that persists today. Adherents of the Doctrine of Signatures claimed that the walnut's head-shaped husk and brain-like kernel would 'comfort the brain and head mightily'. A strong infusion of walnut leaves is said to deter ants.

Watercress

Nasturtium officinale

Scurvy grass

Habitat Native to Europe. Introduced and naturalized in North America and throughout the world. Found in ditches, at the sides of streams and in moist meadows watered by springs. Cultivated commercially in beds as a salad vegetable.
Description Aquatic, hardy perennial with succulent, hollow, branching stems from 30–60cm (1–2ft). The creeping or floating stems root easily and bear fleshy, shiny, heart-shaped leaves. The leaves are very dark green to brownish green or bronze, with a distinctive bitter taste. From early summer to mid-autumn, clusters of small white flowers appear at the tips of the stems. **Parts used**: leafy stems.
History From the earliest times, watercress has been valued as both a food and a medicine. The plant is rich in vitamin C and iron, and is one of the oldest remedies for scurvy. Hippocrates considered watercress a digestive stimulant and prescribed it for coughs. Herbalists still recommend the herb for catarrh and bronchitis, and also for skin problems since it helps the body to eliminate wastes.

Commercially grown watercress is grown in prepared beds fed by clean, running water. The wild plant, however, may grow in still water of questionable quality and carry deadly parasites. It was once a common source of typhoid infection. Watercress is a valuable winter salad vegetable but large doses are purgative.
Growing tips Watercress is easily propagated from cuttings left to root in water. It requires rich, very moist soil and frequent watering.

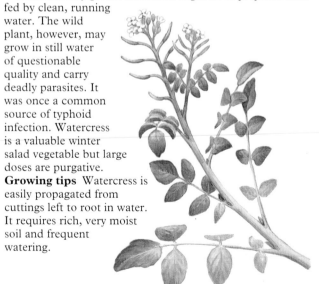

White Horehound

LABIATAE

Marrubium vulgare

Habitat Native to central and southern Europe, western Asia, and North Africa. Naturalized in Britain and North America. Found on field edges, waste ground, and rough pastureland, on dry, sandy or chalky soil.

Description Branching, bushy, perennial with erect, square stems from 60–90cm (2–3ft), and bearing some resemblance to catnip. The whole plant is covered in whitish hairs giving it a woolly appearance. The leaves are arranged in opposite pairs up the stem and are rounded to oval in shape with dentate margins. They are faintly aromatic, with downy, wrinkled upper surfaces. Whorls of numerous white, tubular flowers bloom towards the top of the stem throughout the summer.

Part used: flowering plant.

History White horehound contains a bitter principle, and was one of the bitter herbs eaten by the Jews at Passover. *Har hune* means hairy plant in Old English and is thought to be the origin of the plant's common name, horehound.

Today white horehound is valued for its expectorant properties and has long been one of the principal herbal remedies for chest complaints. Horehound tea and cough mixtures were popular from the beginning of the 17th century, and horehound candy was a favourite household remedy for coughs. Emigrants from England took the plant to North America and horehound cough preparations were popular with the Shakers. A hot infusion of the leaves also promotes sweating, and is a folk remedy for feverish colds.

Wild Carrot

Daucus carota

Queen Anne's Lace, bird's nest

Habitat Native to Europe, also North Africa, and western Asia. Found wild in hedgerows, pastureland and field edges, especially near the coast.

Description Biennial on a thin, white, very fibrous root. The furrowed, hairy stems grow from 60–90cm (2–3ft) and bear feathery, dark green leaves with sheathed bases. From mid-summer dense, flattened terminal umbels of creamy white flowers appear, with a central deep purple flower.

Parts used: leaves and dried seeds.

History Carrot leaf tea was drunk for bladder complaints.

Wild Yam

Dioscorea villosa

Colic root

Habitat Native to North America from Rhode Island southwards to Florida. Vine that grows in thickets and hedges, and over fences.

Description Perennial vine with slender, tuberous, knotted rootstock and twining, woody stems that are reddish brown and grow from 1.5m–4.5m (5–15ft). The broad leaves are oval to heart-shaped and smooth in texture. Small yellowish-green flowers appear from early to mid-summer on drooping stems. **Part used:** root.

History A traditional remedy for menstrual cramps and colic.

Willow

Salix alba and spp.

White willow

Habitat Native to Europe and introduced into northern temperate zones, including North America. Found along the banks of rivers and streams, and in wet meadows, often near habitation. More common as an ornamental.

Description Tall, graceful tree to 20m (65ft) with greyish-brown, deeply fissured bark. The long, steeply angled branches are obscured by distinctive silvery blue-green, narrow, tapering leaves that curl at the tip. In spring drooping, bright yellow male catkins appear. The fruiting female catkins are initially green then turn white and fluffy. **Part used**: bark.

History Willow bark has been used since the first century AD to reduce pain and inflammation. The tree also has an ancient reputation in folk medicine for reducing the temperature in fevers. In the 1820s the active ingredient responsible for willow's medicinal properties, which is also found in meadowsweet, was isolated and named salicin, after the *Salix* genus. Around 70 years later, after salicin had been synthesized into salicylic acid, the drug aspirin was formulated and marketed. Willow bark also contains astringent tannins and has been used medicinally for heartburn.

According to medieval folklore, witches used willow to treat rheumatism and fever, and the old word for witches, wicca, may be the origin of the term wicker, applied to baskets woven from willow twigs. 'Pussy willows', the fluffy silvery grey catkins, were reputed to turn into witches' cats. In Elizabethan England, wearing a sprig of willow in your hat signified rejection by a loved one.

Wintergreen

Gaultheria procumbens

Mountain tea

Habitat Native to eastern North America from Canada
southwards to Georgia. Grows in open woodland at the base
of trees and in clearings, providing ground cover.
Description Evergreen shrub with creeping, woody branches
to 15cm (6in) that bears tufts of oval bright green leaves.
These are glossy above and paler beneath, leathery in texture,
and with serrated margins. Nodding, bell-shaped white flowers
with five petals appear in mid-summer, followed by scarlet,
edible berries. **Parts used**: leaves and oil.
History Wintergreen is a traditional Native American remedy
for aching and arthritic limbs. The leaves were pounded and
made into a poultice to soothe painful joints and also to
alleviate inflammations and swellings. Taken internally, a tea
of the leaves was considered a cure for fever, sore throats and
stomach inflammations.

Wintergreen leaves have a pleasant menthol flavour and
they were a popular substitute for expensive, imported Indian
tea. Wintergreen oil, present in the
leaves and berries, contains
methyl salicylate, a pain- and
inflammation-relieving compound.
It makes a soothing rub
for strained muscles
and joints
and commercially
produced
preparations
for strains and
sports injuries are
often based on
wintergreen oil.
In the USA,
where
wintergreen
is known
as teaberry, it
is used to flavour
chewing
gum and
toothpaste.

Witch hazel

HAMAMELIDACEAE

Hamamelis virginiana

Snapping hazelnut

Habitat Native to North America except the far west. Found in damp, open woods and along stream banks from Nova Scotia eastwards to Minnesota and southwards to Georgia. Grown as an ornamental in parks and gardens, witch hazel is also cultivated commercially.

Description Deciduous, spreading shrub or small tree from 2.5–4.6m (8–15ft) forking into several long, crooked branches that are covered in smooth greyish-brown bark. The leaves are elliptical to obovate in shape with unevenly scalloped edges and roughish undersides. They are downy when young and turn a luminous yellow in autumn. When the leaves fall, the tree bears clusters of bright yellow flowers with four, narrow, strip-like petals and yellowish-brown interiors. These are followed by nut-like seed capsules that do not ripen until the following autumn. **Parts used**: bark, leaves and twigs.

History Witch hazel's flexible forked twigs have long been used for water divining purposes. The English name is derived from an Anglo-Saxon word, wic-en, meaning to bend, but this may have been confused with wicca, an old name for witches. Medieval witch hunters were, however, equipped with hazel rods.

Witch hazel bark, twigs and leaves contain astringent tannins that reduce inflammation and stem bleeding. Native American Indians applied witch hazel poultices to ease swellings and ulcers, while witch hazel tea was drunk as a tonic and to relieve mouth ulcers and inflamed throats. Herbalists consider witch hazel an excellent remedy for haemorrhoids and varicose veins, as well as cuts and bruises. Today, distilled witch hazel is a common first-aid remedy found in many household medicine cabinets.

Woodruff

RUBIACEAE

Asperula odorata or *Galium odoratum*

Sweet woodruff

Habitat Native to Europe, Asia, and North Africa, and introduced elsewhere. Cultivated in the USA. Found wild in woods, especially beech woods, and shady banks and hedgerows spots on moist, loamy soil.

Description Perennial with erect, smooth, slender stems to 25cm (10in) with whorls of six to nine leaves arranged at intervals along them, like the spokes of a wheel. The narrow leaves are dark green and lance-shaped with rough edges. From early summer small, white, tubular flowers bloom in loose clusters, followed by bristly seed balls, like cleavers. When fresh, the plant is odourless; when dried it smells of new-mown hay. **Part used**: dried flowering plant.

History In Medieval times, dried woodruff was widely employed as a strewing herb, and its fresh, hay-like scent made it a popular mattress stuffing. In parts of Germany, woodruff, with a little brandy and sugar, is still a flavouring for sharp new wine. This traditional drink is known as the 'May bowl' and has been served to welcome the spring since the 13th century. Steep fresh woodruff in white wine for a subtle vanilla flavour.

In the Middle Ages, fresh woodruff leaves were applied to cuts and wounds, and a tea was drunk to ease stomach cramps. Today, the herb is rarely employed by medical herbalists and the US Food and Drug Administration consider it safe for use only in alcoholic drinks. Taken in large quantities, the herb may cause vomiting and dizziness.

Growing tips Woodruff is very slow to germinate. Sow seed in autumn in moist, well-drained, rich soil in the shade.

Wormwood

Artemisia absinthium

Absinthe

Habitat Native to the Mediterranean and central Europe. Introduced to North America from Newfoundland south to Montana. Naturalized in temperate zones. Grows wild on roadsides and waste ground.

Description Shrubby, spreading, very aromatic perennial to 75cm (2.5ft) with hairy stems and greyish, pinnate leaves that are deeply divided into narrow, blunt-ended segments. The leaves are dark green and covered in silky, greyish hairs: the undersides are also downy. From mid-summer to mid-autumn, small, globular, greenish-yellow flowers appear on slender, erect stalks. **Part used**: flowering plant.

History Wormwood has been used medicinally to expel intestinal worms for over 3500 years. *Absinthium*, the plant's specific name, denotes the traditional and most celebrated use of wormwood – in the potent French drink, absinthe, reputedly first prepared by witches. However, absinthe has been banned from most countries owing to its habit-forming nature and dangerous effects, including convulsions. Wormwood is also used to flavour vermouth.

Wormwood is an old remedy for stomach ailments. Its bitterness helps to improve a poor appetite and alleviates a wide range of digestive problems. Externally, a compress of the leaves was applied to painful rheumatic joints, to stimulate poor circulation, and also to hasten childbirth.

In the home, wormwood was a traditional insect repellant, and was strewn over floors and placed among clothes and linen. For its bitter taste, wormwood was used in brewing beer before the advent of hops.

Woundwort

Stachys palustris

Marsh woundwort, clown's woundwort, all-heal

Habitat Native to Europe and common in Britain in marshy meadows, and by rivers, streams and ditches. Widely distributed in northern temperate zones.

Description Nettle-like perennial with stout, quadrangular stems from 60–90cm (2–3ft) and long-stalked basal leaves that wither before flowering. The oblong, lance-shaped leaves have rounded bases that clasp the stem and taper to a narrow point. They are arranged in pairs up the stem, and both leaves and stem are hairy. From late summer spikes of mauve, two-lipped, mottled flowers bloom in whorls of six at the tip of the stem. **Parts used**: leaves and flowering stems.

History Woundwort, also known as all-heal, enjoyed a considerable reputation as a healer from the Middle Ages onwards. A poultice of the fresh leaves was applied to cuts and wounds, and the celebrated herbalist Gerard claimed to have 'cured many grievous wounds, and some mortale with the same herb'.

Woundwort has long been a traditional remedy for cramp, gout and painful joints, due to its antispasmodic action. Herbalists still prescribe the herb for cramping pains and attribute the herb's success as a wound healer to its astringent and antiseptic properties. In folk medicine direct application of fresh woundwort leaves is still recommended for cuts and wounds, while woundwort tea is thought to be helpful for diarrhoea.

Yarrow

Achillea millefolium

Milfoil, soldier's woundwort, carpenter's weed, nosebleed

Habitat Native to Europe and naturalized in North America and temperate zones. Common in pastures, on embankments, roadsides and waste ground.

Description Perennial with an erect, rough, angular stem to 90cm (3ft) with attractive, feathery foliage. The very finely cut leaves clasp the stem towards the top, while the lower leaves are stalked. Both leaves and stem are covered in fine white hairs. Throughout the summer numerous, small, daisy-like flowers bloom in flat-topped clusters. They are usually white but may be tinged with pink. **Parts used**: flowering stems.

History The ancient Chinese threw yarrow stalks when consulting the celebrated book of divination, the I Ching, and employed the herb medicinally. The Greeks knew of its healing properties and the herb may have been named *Achillea* after Achilles, who reputedly staunched the wounds of his soldiers with yarrow leaves.

The English common names, soldier's woundwort and carpenter's weed, are testimony to yarrow's great reputation as a domestic wound healer. Its astringency helps to stem the flow of blood, and yarrow was still being used to treat soldiers' wounds during the American Civil War. Yarrow leaves were also inserted into the nostrils to stop bleeding, hence its country name nosebleed. Several Native American tribes applied the herb to cuts, wounds and bruises, and drank yarrow tea for fevers and sickness. Yarrow also promotes sweating and hot yarrow tea is a traditional home remedy of long standing for severe colds. Herbalists consider yarrow a valuable remedy for feverish colds and flu, often in combination with elderflower and peppermint.

Yellow Dock

Rumex crispus

Curled dock

Habitat Native to Europe and
naturalized in North America.
Widely distributed in temperate
zones. A common weed in fields,
ditches, and on roadsides.
Description Perennial on stout,
spindle-shaped taproot that is
brown externally and yellowish
inside. The slender stem from
30–90cm (1–3ft) bears oblong to
lance-shaped light green leaves with wavy
edges. The lower leaves may be over 30cm
(1ft) in length. Throughout the summer numerous small
greenish or reddish flowers bloom in whorls along the
upper stem. **Part used**: root.
History Herbalists value the cleansing and mildly laxative
action of yellow dock root in the treatment of skin complaints.

Yellow Jessamine

Gelsemium sempervirens

Yellow jasmine root, Carolina jasmine

Habitat Native to the southern
USA, Mexico and Guatemala.
Found in damp woods and
thickets from Virginia southwards
to Texas and Florida. Cultivated
as an ornamental.
Description Perennial, twining,
evergreen vine with woody, purple-
brown rhizomes and slender, woody
stems to 6m (20ft). These attach
themselves to trees, climbing from
one to the other, and bear lance-shaped,
glossy, dark green leaves. From early to late
spring clusters of sweet-smelling, funnel-shaped yellow
flowers appear. **Parts used**: dried rhizome and root.
History Used in homeopathic dosage for colds and flu.

Index

Aconite 8
Agrimony 9
Alfalfa 10
Allspice 11
Almond 12
Aloe 13
Amaranth 14
American Cranesbill 15
Angelica 16
Aniseed 17
Arnica 18
Arrowroot 19
Asparagus 19
Avens 20

Balm 21
Balmony 22
Barberry 23
Basil 24
Bay 25
Bayberry 26
Bearberry 27
Belladonna 28
Bergamot 29
Bethroot 30
Betony 31
Bistort 31
Black Root 33
Blackberry 32
Bladderwrack 33
Blessed Thistle 34
Blood Root 35
Blue Cohosh 35
Blue Flag 36
Bogbean 36
Boneset 37
Borage 38
Broom 39
Burdock 40

Caraway 41
Carrot, Wild 182
Cascara Sagrada 42
Catnip 43
Cayenne 44
Celandine, Lesser 45
Celery, Wild 46
Centaury 47
Chamomile, German 48; Roman 49
Chervil 50
Chickweed 51
Chicory 52
Chives 53
Cinquefoil 54

Cleavers 54
Coltsfoot 55
Comfrey 56
Coriander 57
Corn Silk 58
Couch Grass 58
Costmary 59
Cowslip 60

Dandelion 61
Dill 62
Dog Rose 64
Dog's Mercury 63
Dyer's Greenweed 65

Echinacea 66
Elder 67
Elecampane 68
Eucalyptus 69
Evening Primrose 70
Eyebright 71

Fennel 72
Fenugreek 73
Feverfew 74
Figwort 75
Flax 76
Foxglove 77
Fringe Tree 78
Fumitory 78

Garlic 79
Gentian, Yellow 80
Ginger 81
Ginseng, American 83; Oriental 82
Golden Seal 84
Goldenrod 83
Gravelroot 85

Hawthorn 86
Hemlock 87
Henbane 88
Henna 89
Hops 90
Horehound, White 181
Horse Chestnut 91
Horseradish 92
Horsetail 93
Hyssop 94

Iceland Moss 95
Iris, Florentine 96
Irish Moss 95

Jimson Weed 97
Juniper 98

Lady's Bedstraw 99
Lady's Mantle 100
Lavender 101
Lemon 102
Lettuce 103
Lily of the Valley 104
Lime 105
Liquorice 106
Lobelia 107
Lovage 108
Lungwort 109

Mace 126
Mandrake 110
Marigold 111
Marjoram, Sweet 112; Wild/
    Oregano 113
Marshmallow 114
Meadowsweet 115
Mint, Peppermint 116
Mistletoe 118
Motherwort 119
Mountain Grape 119
Mugwort 120
Mullein, Great 121
Mustard, Black 122; White 123

Nasturtium 124
Nettle 125
Nutmeg 126

Oak 127
Oats 128
Olive 129

Pansy, Wild 130
Parsley 131
Parsley Piert 132
Pasque Flower 133
Passionflower 134
Pennyroyal 135
Pepper 136
Periwinkle 137
Peruvian Bark 138
Plantain 139
Pleurisy Root 140
Poke Root 140
Pomegranate 141
Poppy 142
Prickly Ash 143
Pumpkin 144
Purslane 145
Pyrethrum 146

Quassia 146

Raspberry 147
Rosemary 148

Rowan 149
Rue 150

Saffron 151
Sage 152–3; Clary 153; Red 153
Sarsaparilla 155
Sassafras 155
Saw Palmetto 156
Self-Heal 157
Senna 158
Shepherd's Purse 159
Skullcap 160
Skunk Cabbage 160
Slippery Elm 161
Soapwort 162
Solomon's Seal 163
Sorrel 164
Southernwood 165
Spearmint 117
Squaw Vine 166
St John's Wort 154
Stone Root 166
Summer Savory 167
Sunflower 168
Sweet Cicely 169
Sweet Violet 170

Tansy 171
Tarragon 172
Thuja 173
Thyme 174

Valerian 175
Verbena, Lemon 176
Vervain 177
Virginia Snakeroot 178

Walnut 179
Watercress 180
Willow 183
Wintergreen 184
Witch Hazel 185
Woodruff 186
Wormwood 187
Woundwort 188

Yam, Wild 182
Yarrow 189
Yellow Dock 190
Yellow Jessamine 190